A Guide on:

How to Protect Your Personal Information

Sandra Raby, M.Ed.
and
Lisa Ruggeri, MAOM

www.personalinfoprotection.com

Bloomington, IN authorHOUSE® Milton Keynes, UK

AuthorHouse™
1663 Liberty Drive, Suite 200
Bloomington, IN 47403
www.authorhouse.com
Phone: 1-800-839-8640

AuthorHouse™ UK Ltd.
500 Avebury Boulevard
Central Milton Keynes, MK9 2BE
www.authorhouse.co.uk
Phone: 08001974150

First published by AuthorHouse 9/25/2006

ISBN: 1-4259-6468-0 (sc)

Library of Congress Control Number: 2006908204

Printed in the United States of America
Bloomington, Indiana

This book is printed on acid-free paper.

In Loving Memory

Thane Emrys Roberts

April 1 – June 6, 2006

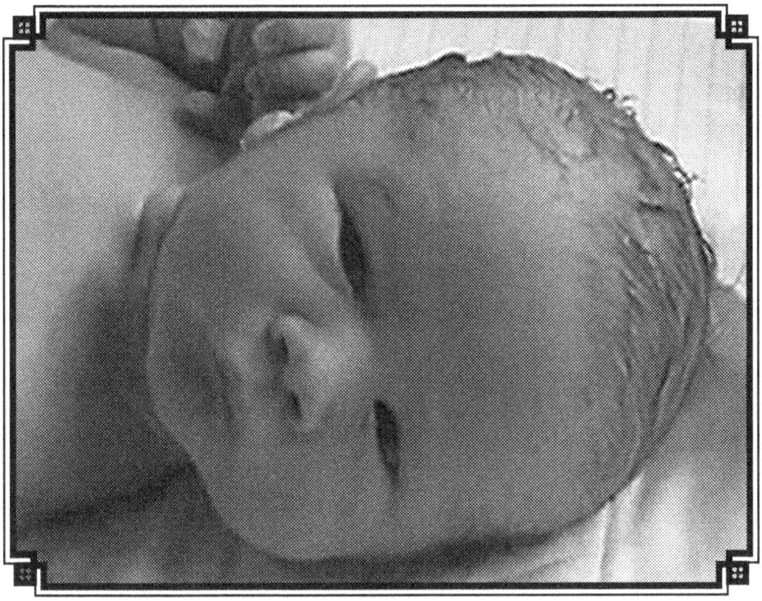

We Love You!

We Miss You!

We Will Never Forget!

The Baby Thane Foundation:

A Non-Profit Organization for Shaken Baby Awareness

www.babythane.com

We would like to dedicate this book to
all the Police Officers, Fire Fighters and
Military members of the United States.

Because of the sacrifices you make every day,
our nation is a safer and better place to live.

Thank you for all your hard work and dedication. This
book was written for each and every one you, for
your personal safety and the safety of your family.

A special thank you goes out to Sandra and Lisa's
police department's officers. Providing you with our
training and your attentiveness to go out and start
the protection process, we have learned just as much
from you as you have from us. No matter where life's
path takes us in the future, you will always hold
a special place in our lives and hearts. Thank you
for what you do on the job each and every day.

We would also like to recognize and thank Detectives
BL, MM and AS for all your hard work and dedication.
Without you and what you have gone through, we
would not have been able to do this project. May
each of you and your families always be safe!

Table of Contents

A Guide on: How to Protect Your Personal Information.

Preface

This book was written as a combined effort by Sandra Raby and Lisa Ruggeri. They both work for a major city police department. Sandra is currently a Police Sergeant and has worked with her agency for 23 years. Lisa is a Criminal Intelligence Analyst and has been working in that capacity for 15 years. They love their jobs and have selected career paths they both enjoy. Sandra and Lisa started to work together in 2005 when they began presenting training classes to their department's police officers on how to protect their personal identifying information from being released into public record and publicly available information sources.

Through the course of Sandra and Lisa's assigned duties, they have learned so much about how prevalent it is for businesses and companies to share, sell and release our personal identifying information as well as what it takes to have someone's personal information removed from public record and from publicly available information sources.

The information and strategies they have discovered relevant to this subject matter would best serve our communities if it was compiled into an easy to use reference book that anyone can utilize, but most especially for those individuals who work in the public service professions. It is essential that each and every individual understands the magnitude of what is going on in today's world within the realm of public record.

As Sandra and Lisa provided this training, session after session, they learned a wealth of information from their on-going research and from the students who attended their classes. Most of the officers who sat through this training acted on the suggestions Sandra and Lisa provided on how to start protecting their personal information and the information of their family members. The officers who have embarked on their own journey of protecting their personal information have provided Sandra and Lisa with excellent feedback, both good and bad, based on their experiences as they are working through this process. Each and every officer who has provided Sandra and Lisa with feedback has assisted them with the research that makes writing this book possible.

Sandra and Lisa have been very passionate about providing this information to their co-workers. They not only realize how beneficial the information contained in this book has been to their department personnel, but also how critical it is to this specific community nationwide. Sandra and Lisa would contend that members of the general public will also discover personal benefits from the information and strategies presented in this book.

Sandra and Lisa decided to write this book so they could reach out and share what they have learned with other individuals across the country. Others, who may never have an opportunity to be exposed to this kind of information, now will be able to have access to it so they too can take additional steps toward safeguarding their lives and the lives of their families.

There is not one thing anyone can do that could be considered a cure all for preventing the release of their personal information without major changes taking place within our existing laws. It is Sandra and Lisa's intent to get the word out on how our personal information is shared and released and to provide viable options on what can be done to safeguard our personal information as best as we can.

Both Sandra and Lisa learn something new each and every day they teach a training session, from the students who are out implementing the strategies they have been given or by doing additional research when they are presented with a new scenario. Even once this book goes to publication, they will discover new avenues and ways our personal information is getting released into public record and publicly available information sources. Their hope is to create an awareness about what we do on a daily basis that makes our personal information available to anyone who wants to find it and to offer suggestions on what can be done to stop this process or if not, at least slow it down.

The ideas presented in this book are not all inclusive and are not intended to be a cure all for the protection of our personal information. This book does not include each and every avenue that exists nor does it include every solution to every situation in which our personal information is released. What Sandra and Lisa present in this book is a good foundation and what they would encourage each and everyone of us to do from this point forward, now that we are aware of how our personal information is shared, is that we ask those questions of the businesses and companies we deal with on a daily basis about what they do with our personal information and what we can do to make them stop.

The process of protecting our personal information will be a lifestyle change for us and our families. For each of us to be successful, we will need to constantly be aware of and monitor how and with whom we conduct our personal business in our daily lives.

Note from Lisa

I want to take a moment to thank those very special people in my life. In writing a book, it takes precious time away from family and friends. I am so thankful that I have a very supportive family, absolutely wonderful friends and the most precious children in my life. I am who I am today with each and every one of you. I want to thank my savior Jesus for the words and wisdom to write this book. I am grateful for the insight to do this project and for the opportunity to get the word out there. I pray that one day I can give back to you all you have blessed me with. I pray this book will allow me to do that.

To my absolutely beautiful children, I love each and every one of you. You are all very important to me. Thank you for enhancing my life. Christopher, right now you are exploring your independent life. We all learn from making choices which ones are right and which ones are wrong. I pray that you learn from the wrong choices and make good decisions so you can love and enjoy life to the fullest. You will always be my son. Kraig, my only natural born son. You are and forever will be my heart and soul. Your smiling face brings the sunshine into my life each and every day. Thank you for allowing me to love other children and not keeping me all to yourself. You are a wonderful young man, I am so proud of you and who you are becoming. Michael, you are so smart and a precious jewel to me. We have been through some times together, but through it all I still have you and am very thankful. I have enjoyed watching you grow into the incredible young man you are. Matthew, I find myself pausing and smiling each time I think of you. You have touched my life and world in ways you will never know. I hold you close and cherish each time with you. We have also been through some rough times, you are a wonderful young man keep your focus and do not let what has happened get you down in life. You are better than that and can rise above it to be a very strong man with a wonderful life. Mandi, my most precious niece and my only girl. You are so fun to be around, I cherish all our girl times together. I love it when your giggles fill my house. You are a beautiful young woman and I look forward to many more girl times with you. Riley, you have had a special place in my heart from the moment I met you back when you were three. Your face, laughter and personality brighten up my day. I am very thankful for you and that I did not loose you. Liam, you are a true miracle from God. You came when I needed a touch of God himself. Thank you for letting me be your Ga Ma Ga (God mommy), this is the most precious job in all the earth. I cherish each and every moment with you. You too, have become my heart and soul. Thanks for all the sugars. Thane, our precious little baby Thane. You too were a blessing from God. I will forever cherish the two months we had you. I will hold true to my promise to take care of your mommy and your big brother forever. I love you, I miss you and I will never forget. Changes will take place in your memory on Shaken Baby Syndrome, please visit www.babythane.com. To all the other beautiful children in my life, I am blessed having you as well; Nicholas, Lauren, David, Toni, Angela, Brianna, Alex, Zachary, Bradley, and Lisa.

I want to thank all my girlfriends, with out you I could not be who I am today. Thank you for all your love and support I receive from you each and every day. Time was taken away from you in writing this book. I am thankful that you recognize the importance of this project and the support you have given me. A girl is nothing with out her girls; Anna, Annette, Christy, Diane, Dottie, Erin, Fran, Jacqui, Jennifer, Jennifer, Jessica, Julie, Kathryn, Kelly, Kris, Libby, my twin Lisa R, Maria, Melissa, Meri-Le, Pam, Rebecca, Renee, Robin, Sandra, Sarah, Sharon, Shelly, Sonja, Tina, Wendy. Then there are my guy friends, I would never forget you as you all hold a place in my heart as well; Andy, Bob, Bob, Darren, Greg, John, Keith, Matt, Mike, Kelly, Ritchie. I also want to thank my parents, Donna and Gene for all their love and support over the years. I want to thank my church family at Scottsdale Worship Center. I feel right at home there with all of you and cherish our times together. Thank you to Pastor Jim and Suzy; Pastor Chris and Jennifer; Pastor Mike and Rebekah; Pastor Lenny and Mariam; Pastor Jason and Jelynda; Pastor Ed and Julie; Barry and Mary; John and Kim; Phil and Kim; Gail, Rick.

Note from Sandra

I will never be able to name all those individuals who have played a part in the success of this book. The family, friends, acquaintances, and life experiences that have allowed me to accomplish this tremendous undertaking at this point in time have not gone unnoticed. Writing this book has been demanding of my time and attention which my family has graciously tolerated. I know every day they have felt my absence. Thank you, Mary Lou, for putting up with me being distracted.

I would be remiss; however, if I did not take the time to acknowledge those individuals who, over time, have impacted my life, helping make me the person I am today. First, for my Dad and his wife, Darlene - Pops, early on, I know you had your doubts about me, but I hope I have shown you that I am someone you can be proud of. I do appreciate the things you have done for me as I know it was not easy for you to take on all three of us by yourself. Darlene, thank you for becoming a part of the family and most especially, for being able to put up with the "Raby" attitude for as long as you have. It truly takes a special person to deal with all of us and still keep their sanity. To my sister, Diane – you were right when you said "all that matters is you're my sister". Thank you for not being judgmental and always being there. I wish you all the happiness in the world because you are most deserving. And you always find the best birthday cards! I would also like to acknowledge my Grandma and Grandpa Raby. I know they are constantly watching me from the other side, smiling down on me, helping me celebrate my successes. You are always with me in my heart.

To call someone a friend is something that is very important and significant to me. There are so few who I will actually call my friend. Because of the special place my friends do have in my life, I need to call them out – Sharon, Barbara, Carol, Heidi, and Tom. You have stood by me through thick and thin, good and bad. Even if you didn't agree with me, you voiced your opinion but never left my side. Distance and relationships have never driven a wedge between us. I will be forever grateful for the insight and wisdom you have shared with me. Each of you has a special place in my heart and I hope you know how important and special you are to me. Thank you for being a part of my life!

Last, but certainly not least, I need to thank my baby, Leilani, who is my angel from heaven, for coming into my life. You are truly a gift from God and have taught me what life is really all about. For only having been on this earth for three years, you are a very wise soul. I have learned so much from you during the short amount of time we have been together. I love you and will always be your mommy angel....forever.

PART I: HOW AND WHY PERSONAL INFORMATION IS RELEASED INTO PUBLIC RECORD.

Introduction

This book has been designed so that each chapter gradually builds on the previous chapters. There is so much to learn and understand about what is going on in the realm of public record that it is best if we take it one step at a time. Everyone needs to understand what is public record, how and why our personal identifying information is getting out in public record, who is sharing, selling, and releasing our personal identifying information, who is buying it, the laws regarding this type of activity, the steps we, as consumers, can take to protect ourselves and control what information is being released, what role the Internet is playing in the availability of public record, and what steps can be taken to protect ourselves from identity theft.

Rather than focusing only on identity theft, the main focus of this book will be on preventing our personal identifying information from being shared, sold and released, along with learning about the steps we can take to stop this activity. Protecting our personal information and identity theft do go hand in hand, however, if you take our advice and implement the strategies we suggest on how to protect your personal information, the probability of becoming an identity theft victim will be greatly reduced. The chances of becoming a victim will never completely be eliminated, but at least you will be on top of the situation which will enable you to recognize any discrepancies early on, allowing you to put a stop to this illegal activity before it completely takes over your entire life.

In addition to the many strategies we will suggest, we have also included a check list at the end of the book that will assist you with implementing our suggestions. Utilizing this check list will make it easier for you to start the process of protecting your personal information.

CHAPTER 1: WHAT IS PUBLIC RECORD INFORMATION?

What is Considered Public Record?

If you go to www.google.com and type in "public record information", you will receive 197,000,000 responses. Click into some of the websites that are identified in the responses, run your name, and read about what public records are.

We clicked into the first website that came up, www.LocatePublicRecords.com, and clicked into their "Terms & Conditions" located at the bottom of their home page. After they thank you for visiting their website, they proceed to tell you that they collect your personal identifying information with your consent only. Most of us probably had no idea our information was gathered and made available on this website. It is not just this website that operates in this manner. There are numerous other Internet websites that act as search engines, collecting public record and publicly available information and putting what they gather into a database that can be accessed and queried by anyone who has a computer with an Internet connection.

We need to understand what is considered public record and publicly available information, which government agencies, non-government sources and private businesses collect this information, and what they do with the information once they have it. We also need to understand that the sharing and selling of our personal information is a common business practice between businesses and companies and we need to learn what options are available to us so we can put a stop to this vicious cycle.

Many definitions and various arguments exist about what is considered public record information. The definition of "public record" has changed over the years due largely in part to the invention of the

Internet. In researching public record definitions, the most common theme identified in a majority of them has to do with the records that are maintained by government offices and agencies located in every state throughout America. These government offices' primary function is to store our records while operating under the assumption that the records they maintain are considered "public record" which makes them open to public inspection. Because the information contained in these records is open to public inspection, another main function of these government agencies is to make the information available to anyone who makes a request for it.

Our records housed by public offices have always been considered public record, but with the explosion of the Internet, our records are now available on-line to anyone that has a computer with Internet access. All someone has to do is sit in the comfort of their own home and query any number of available government websites to obtain personal identifying information on any individual of their choosing.

Before the Internet, a person would have to physically make an appearance at one of these government offices that stores our information and submit a public record request, usually done in writing, to obtain the information they were looking for. By utilizing this method, a tracking record was established as to whom was querying particular information housed within a specific set of public records. The Internet has created a veil of anonymity making it much more difficult to track who may be querying specific records, along with having no idea what the person's intent is once they obtain the information they are seeking.

The creation of this veil of anonymity should not only be a major concern for all law enforcement and public service personnel but all American citizens as well. Anyone that has a computer with Internet access can pull up our records that contain our personal identifying information while sitting within the comfort of their own home. There will be no record of these inquiries and when the subject of the search becomes a victim of a crime from information obtained in this way, it will be much more difficult for investigators to conduct any type of follow up.

Due to the multitude of public record sources that are available, we would like to address some specific types of government records that are considered "public record". Keep in mind that there are many other public record sources that are accessible. We are only going to mention the most common record types that are open to public inspection.

Real Estate Deeds

These types of documents are considered one of the main sources of public record information. If you own a home or have owned a home, the paperwork relating to the purchase or sale of your home is considered public record and is filed at your local recorder's office. The information contained in these documents has always been considered public record and is accessible to anyone who makes a request for it. Most recorders' offices are now making the information contained in these documents available on the Internet to include a feature that provides search capabilities within their website.

If your recorder's office puts recorded documents on the Internet, we recommend you access their website and run your name. You will see all of the documents recorded in your name which will include your Deed of Trust, Warranty Deed, and Quit Claim Deeds. These documents are basically all the paperwork you signed when you purchased or sold your home. Within these specific documents, you will find your home address and property's legal description.

The main purpose of every state's recorder's office is for the storage and publication of public record information. At this point in time, the only items we are required to file at the recorder's office are documents regarding the purchase and sales of our homes. If you do not have to file anything at your local recorder's office, please strongly consider not doing so.

While conducting job-related research, we have seen all kinds of documents that have been filed with our county recorder's office that absolutely do not have to be recorded. Once a document is filed at the recorder's office, regardless of the document type, it is then considered public record and there is nothing we can do to have the document removed from public record even if it contains personal identifying information, i.e. – date of birth, social security number, home address, and home phone number. We cannot control the release of this information; however, we can control what information is available to be released. Since it is standard practice for our recorder's office to make recorded documents available on the Internet and if you take a personal document that has no requirement to be recorded and you record it, you will be making the information contained in that document public record available to anyone who might be utilizing the Internet in an attempt to locate your personal information.

We have seen military discharge papers, divorce decrees, marriage certificates, birth certificates, death certificates, and trust related documents recorded on our county recorder's website. It is not necessary to file these documents at the recorder's office. Be advised that some attorneys preparing these types of documents will advise you to record them. Make it a point to ask if it is absolutely necessary and strongly consider not filing the documents if there is no legal requirement to do so.

Lawsuits and Court Records

Any type of criminal or civil court case, to include lawsuits and divorces, filed in a court of record (using Arizona as an example, this would include Municipal Courts, Superior Courts, Appellate Courts, the State Supreme Court and a variety of Federal courts) is also considered public record. Like the recorder's office, it is becoming common practice for most Courts to put their case information available on-line in a searchable format on the Internet. In many instances, a majority of the case information will not be available on the Internet, but there is nothing to preclude someone from going to the court in person and submitting a public record request to obtain the entire case history.

If you have been a party to any type of court case, make sure you search to see if the courts in your state are putting their case information on-line. We recommend you query your name to see what information about you is available. Watch to see if any personal identifying information shows up on the courts' websites. If any of your personal information is available, go to that particular court and fill out the necessary paperwork to have it removed. Generally speaking, the courts will not redact your actual cases but they will remove personal identifying information such as addresses and dates of birth.

Liens

Many types of liens can be filed against us and often times it is done without our knowledge. People will generally file liens at the recorder's office. The most common types of liens we have seen filed are chiropractic liens, medical liens, mechanic liens, and home owner association liens. We recommend you check your local recorder's office periodically to see if anything new has been filed against you.

Professional Licensing Records

Most professional licenses are considered public record and the latest trend for the entities responsible for maintaining, monitoring, and enforcing these licenses is to make this public record information accessible on the Internet. The licensing records we have found that are available via the Internet are for doctors, nurses, a variety of other positions within the medical field, lawyers, real estate agents, pilots, and cosmetologists. In researching what other types of records are available on the Internet, we have been amazed to find that most professions that require a license of some kind make their database available in a searchable format on the Internet.

If you are in an occupation that requires a professional license within your state, you may want to research the entity that issues your license. Determine if the licensing entity is making the licensee's public record information accessible on the Internet. If so, query your name and see if you are listed and exactly what personal identifying information is available on you. You may not be able to control your license information being in a searchable format on the Internet as it is considered public record but check to see if you have any control over the amount of personal identifying information that is released about you, like your home address, phone number, date of birth, and social security number.

Business Entity Filings (Corporations and LLC's)

Corporation papers and other business type filings are also considered public record. Most states are starting to make this public record information available on the Internet as well. Check with your state entity that is responsible for maintaining and monitoring business filings (using Arizona as an example this entity is the Corporation Commission) to see if they are making their database accessible on the Internet. If you are involved with a business or corporation, we recommend you query your name in their on-line database to see exactly what personal identifying information is available on you.

In the past, it was the norm to get a corporation to purchase a house in an attempt to put another layer between the address and the actual homeowner. This was a relatively viable option before the invention of the Internet. Due to the increasing popularity of the Internet, just like the other public record sources we have talked about, corporation and business filing information is now available right at someone's fingertips using their own home computer.

If you are considering a limited liability company, check with your attorney or accountant to see if they are willing to be listed as the company's statutory agent so no other officers or members have to be recorded. This is another available alternative that will help protect your personal identifying information in this public record source and put a level of protection between you and your LLC.

If you establish a corporation, the board of directors will need to be listed on the forms filed with the Corporation Commission (or the entity specific to your state). You need to know that all the documents associated with a corporation are public record so be careful with what address you list in these documents. Because this information is considered public record and available to anyone who asks for it, we recommend you use the business address or a mailing address instead of your home address.

Birth, Death, Divorce, and Marriage Records

Birth and death records are obtained through a state's Office of Vital Statistics. In researching how the different states handle these types of records, we have found that some states are considered "open record" states so the information contained in these documents is considered public record and other states are considered "closed record" states so the information is not available as a public record.

Some of the open record states, such as California, Nevada, Colorado, and Texas, are putting their vital record information on the Internet in a searchable format. We have also found that there are still many "open record" states that do not have their records accessible on the Internet so their information is not searchable in this format, however, this would not preclude someone from making a record request in person.

Arizona is a "closed record" state so the vital record information contained in these types of documents is not considered public record. Check with the vital records office in your state to see if they are considered an "open" or "closed record" state to determine if these types of documents relating to you and your family members are public record or "closed record".

Divorce records, as is the case in Arizona, are maintained by the Clerk of the Superior Court. In Arizona, these cases are considered public record and are available on the Superior Court's website. Many other states are also making this public record information available on the Internet. There will come a point in time when every state will make divorce records available and searchable on the Internet.

As we discussed earlier in the court case section, we recommend you find out if the family court that is handling your divorce is putting case information on-line. If you find your case is available on the Internet to include any of your personal identifying information, go to the court and find out what you need to do to have your personal information made unavailable from public inspection.

Another set of records that some states also consider public record are marriage licenses. The states that do consider these documents public record are making the license information accessible on the Internet. Nevada is one example of a state that considers marriage license information public record and is putting it on-line.

We recommend you research the courts in your state to see what case information is available on the Internet. If you find any of your personal identifying information, you need to go to that particular court and find out what you can do to have it removed from being accessible on-line.

What Personal Information Should be Protected?

There is personal information that is considered by many to be protected, yet when we query ourselves in many of the Internet databases these information items show up. We have to give some thought as to how this personal identifying information becomes available. We also need to start taking some necessary steps to help protect this information from being available for posting on the various Internet websites.

In addition to the traditional sources of public record information maintained by the government, we have also become our own worst enemy. When we willingly give our personal identifying information to third parties, i.e. – companies and businesses we deal with on a daily basis, we make major contributions to the large pool of our personal information that is being made publicly available on the growing number of Internet websites.

Personal identifying information is generally defined as information about a specific individual that uniquely identifies that person or is directly attributed to them. Examples of this type of information include our name, home address, date of birth and home telephone number. Personal identifying information can be found in public records, non-public information, and publicly available information sources.

A good rule of thumb to follow would be to never give out any personal identifying information with out first asking specific questions about what is done with the information, how it is stored at the business, and if the business or company releases or sells it to other businesses. A good example of this practice is the creditors we deal with on a regular basis who need our personal identifying information to extend us credit. To obtain financing, we need to provide our personal information; however, we should also be asking the company we are doing business with what they do with our information once they have it. We need to get in the habit of asking these types of questions up front and then be prepared to do whatever it takes to get the company or business we are dealing with to stop releasing our personal identifying information they collect on us and we provide to them.

By the end of this book, you will not only understand what questions you need to ask to ensure your safety and the protection of your personal information but you will also have some strategies to put into place that will help prevent the release of your personal identifying information into these public record and Internet databases.

Let us briefly discuss in more detail the items described as personal identifying information.

Date of Birth

Our date of birth is considered personal information, yet it is released and sold by businesses and companies. Because we willingly provide this information in many instances, it is considered a releasable item. We should take whatever steps we can to protect this piece of personal identifying information.

Social Security Number

Our Social Security Number should also be highly protected. Not only do we need to protect this information, but our creditors should safeguard it as well. Government entities can only use our social security numbers as outlined in the Privacy Act of 1974. When a government entity asks someone for their social security number, the Privacy Act mandates the entity tell the person what law gives them the authority to ask for the number, whether providing their number is mandatory or voluntary, what will be done with the information once it is given, and what consequences there will be if they refuse to provide their social security number.

We suggest you follow the guidelines presented in the Privacy Act and ask the questions to obtain the information the government is required to provide when they ask for our social security number. Once you have the answers to these questions, your decision to disclose your social security number should be an easier one to make. Unless it is absolutely necessary and required by law, we recommend you never give your social security number out to anyone for any reason.

Home Addresses and Phone Numbers

We also believe that our addresses and home phone numbers should be protected items as well. These are both considered personally identifying information and are included in public record and publicly available information sources. Because we give out our address and phone number to companies and businesses we deal with on a daily basis, it is very difficult to make the argument for an expectation of privacy with these two items thus this information is shared, sold and released by businesses and companies unless we tell them not to.

What Information is Considered Publicly Available?

Publicly available information is generally defined as information specific to an individual that is available to the general public from non-governmental sources. Information sources of this type are newspapers, telephone directories, magazines, and other publications. It is possible that the items described as personal identifying information may be found within publicly available information sources.

Publicly available information will be covered throughout this book. There are things we do on a daily basis that keeps our personal identifying information available in public record and publicly available information sources. Businesses and companies we do business with will take our information and either share, sell or release it. They can legally do this because we willingly provided them with our personal information so we can do our business with them.

We, as consumers, need to have a good understanding of this concept and be willing to take the necessary steps to avoid this from happening. This book's overall focus is on what is considered publicly available information and what we do on a daily basis that keeps our personal identifying information available to the general public.

As with the public record sources, there are many different sources that exist for someone to access and obtain publicly available information on any individual. Again, we are only going to talk about the most common sources for this type of information.

Published Telephone Directories

Telephone directories generally deal with the land line phones we have at our residences. Listings of these numbers are published by the company that provides us with our telephone service. If you do not pay your provider the extra charges for a non-published and non-listed number, your name, home address and phone number will be put in that provider's directory.

The information in these telephone directories is considered publicly available information and will be sold and included in the public record databases that are found on the Internet. Because this information is considered publicly available, it is obtainable by every business and company that asks for it and the information will be sold and re-sold in a continual cycle. We recommend you pay those extra charges so these items of personal identifying information will not be published and sold which will help eliminate an easy avenue for someone to locate you.

Cell phone companies are not currently selling their subscribers' account information. At this point in time, this specific information is not considered public record or publicly available information. For law enforcement to obtain this information legally from cell phone companies, agencies must obtain a search warrant. We do foresee a time when this will change and cell phone customer account information will be considered publicly available information and released.

Many rumors and e-mails have been circulating for years about this exact topic. When it finally does happen that your cell phone company can share, sell and release its customer account information, they will need to contact you about this change in their policies so watch for this notification. At the time this change occurs, the wireless service providers will probably offer us the option to pay those extra charges on our cell phone numbers for non-published and non-listed so our personal identifying information will not be released, published and/or sold. The argument that is being used to prevent the release of cell phone subscriber account information at this point in time is that as long as consumers are paying for their incoming and outgoing calls; the personal information contained in their accounts should remain non-public records.

Private Data Compilers

Private data compilers are businesses that collect information based on a particular company's need. Most of the private data compilers collect data that relates to consumers' spending habits which might include what, where, when and how much the consumer spends. This type of information is gathered through a consumer's credit card usage and the places where the consumer likes to shop. Businesses use the collected information to focus on what the current market trends are like and it helps provide vital information on how the business should market or create new products for future success.

Public Record Custodians

Public record custodians are agencies, both government and non-government, that store documents and information considered public record and publicly available information. We have talked about several thus far to include the states' recorder's office, telephone directories, and Office of Vital Statistics to name just a few.

The primary purpose of these custodians is to store our records and make them available to anyone who submits a request for them. The records housed by these agencies have always been considered public record and publicly available information. Before the Internet's existence, for someone to be able to access these records, they would need to make their request in person at that specific agency office. The invention of the Internet has provided these agencies with an easy avenue to publicize our records making it more convenient for the general public to access information contained within a specific agency's database.

Public record custodians sell and release our personal identifying information. Most of the larger internet databases, as well as many telemarketing companies, will obtain or purchase this information. This is how our personal identifying information gets out on the Internet without our knowledge. Also keep in mind these larger databases will sell the information they obtain to other, often times, smaller databases. Once our information reaches the Internet, the sharing and selling of our personal identifying information is a viscous cycle that is difficult to stop.

What is Considered Non-Public Information?

Non-public information is another source we need to be aware of that contains our personal identifying information. These sources of information are usually privately owned and not available to the general public. Non-public information sources may include items such as your name, date of birth, your social security number, current and previous addresses as well as previous names used. Non-public information generally has more restrictive release guidelines. The businesses that maintain non-public information will only release items to law enforcement, government agencies, law firms and other commercial and professional users for the purpose of locating individuals or verifying information provided by the individuals they are dealing with.

Let us review a few of the most common non-public record sources. Throughout the rest of this book, we will discuss several of these areas in more detail as we need to understand that within each information source, personal identifying items may be accessible as public record and/or as non-public record information.

Financial Data Contained Within our Credit Reports

The financial information contained within our credit reports is considered non-public information. This financial data generally includes the financial institutions we do business with along with our account numbers and other bank and credit information.

When we go to make a purchase and want to use credit to do so, the institution we are requesting the financing through can not access our financial information from our credit reports without our consent. We need to sign a form that grants them permission to access and view the financial information contained in our credit reports.

Credit reports will be covered in more detail in Chapters 3 and 7. The important thing we need to understand, at this point, is that only our financial information maintained by the credit bureaus is considered non-public record information.

Tax Records

Our tax records maintained by the IRS and our local state tax agencies are also considered non-public record information. Tax records will usually contain our financial information to include our income and the sources of our income.

Employment Information

Our employment histories and information is also considered non-public record information. The companies, businesses, organizations, and agencies we work for may be contacted for employment verification; however, they should not release any of our personal identifying information.

On the other hand, various items contained in our personnel files may be considered public record. Some examples of these items would be awards, performance evaluations, and disciplinary notices.

Bank Information

Our financial institutions also regard our personal information as non-public record information. Financial institutions include banks and credit unions. Our account and financial data is protected, however, we must always ask our financial institutions those important questions about when do they share, sell and release our personal identifying information.

If you only maintain a checking and a savings account with a bank or credit union, they will not release your personal and account information. Once you apply for a loan from your bank or credit union and they extend you credit, they will begin releasing and selling your personal identifying information, i.e. - your name, home address and telephone number. Usually, our financial institutions make opt-out forms available so their customers can request their personal identifying information not be shared, sold or released.

CHAPTER 2: THE RELEASE OF OUR PERSONAL IDENTIFYING INFORMATION

The ideas presented in this chapter are very important for all of us to understand. If you do not learn anything else from reading this book, the one thing, as a minimum, you should take away with you is that businesses and companies we do business with every day make more money selling our personal information than they do having us as customers. Businesses are making over 2 billion (yes billion) dollars a year selling our information. A majority of the time, we do not even know companies and businesses are engaged in this activity.

We have identified some strategies that can be implemented to help prevent the release of our personal information. It is important for us to understand that this is a common business practice throughout corporate America. Who are these companies that engage in this activity? Name any company you deal with and we would venture to guess that they are involved with the release of your information to some degree – some more and some less than others. If we were to name just a few of these companies and businesses, they would include our creditors, the places we order pizza from, the stores we shop at weekly, and the websites we seek out on the Internet.

This chapter is an overview on what is taking place within corporate America in regards to the release of our personal information. We want you to have a basic understanding of the topics that are presented in this chapter. We will cover many of the ideas in greater detail in future chapters. Throughout this book, we will continually provide you with strategies you can implement that will help you start protecting your personal information. These strategies will include steps you can take to get businesses and companies to stop sharing and releasing your personal information.

Why Businesses Release our Information?

It is all about the **MONEY**! And lots of it too! Companies and businesses share our personal information for a variety of reasons. Some of the more common reasons include as a way to offer us more services, introduce us to new services and products, and to make money on the information they already have about us. If we do not tell these companies and businesses that we do not want them to share, sell or release our personal information, they will continue to do so and make a hefty profit in the process. Remember...this is a 2 billion dollar industry!

As a general rule, businesses and companies that engage in financial type activities are required to send their customers a copy of their privacy policy at least once a year. We recommend that you get in the habit of reading these notices when you receive them because, within this privacy policy, it will explain how that particular company handles and shares your personal identifying information. These notices will also contain specific instructions on what you can do to safeguard your personal identifying information maintained by the company in question, more commonly referred to as "opting out". If we do not follow the opt-out procedures outlined in these privacy notices, any of our personal information we provide to that business to include our name, date of birth, social security number, home address and phone number, we are silently giving them permission to share, sell or release it.

There are Federal laws in place that try to balance the consumer's right to privacy with the company's right to conduct their day to day business operations. If the company you are doing business with indicates within its privacy policy that they will only share your personal information as required by law, than you will not have any opt-out choices available from this company. On the other hand, if the company describes within its privacy policy the ways it shares and releases your personal information, than the company is required to provide you the right to opt-out of some of their sharing practices.

Opt-out rights apply when a company shares our information with other businesses that generally fall within two categories, affiliates and non-affiliates. Affiliates are generally described as other companies that are within the same corporate group and non-affiliates are those companies that are not. We recommend if a company you are doing business with states in its privacy policy that it shares your personal information under any other circumstances except as permitted by law that you follow whatever opt-out process they set forth and exercise your right to opt-out under every available option.

One of the main reasons why we will never be able to completely stop the dissemination of our personal information by companies and businesses we deal with is because the Federal privacy laws allow the companies that engage in financial activities to share certain types of our personal information without giving us the right to opt-out. Some of the circumstances in which companies can share our information with their non-affiliates include giving it to other businesses that help market and promote their own products, our transaction records to other businesses they contract with to service our account/s, in response to a court order or subpoena, and providing our payment history to the credit bureaus.

We need to understand that all businesses and companies will share, sell or release our personal information in varying degrees. Once we know this, we need to start asking the businesses and companies we deal with on a regular basis questions about their release practices and determine if we have the right to opt-out so we can start limiting the release of our personal information.

Every business will have a privacy policy. During your dealings with any particular company, you should be provided a copy of their privacy policy at different times throughout your relationship with them. When you initially become one of their customers, you should receive a copy of their policy. Every financial institution that you do business with is required to provide you a copy of their privacy policy on an annual basis. If a financial institution that you have dealings with makes a change to their privacy policy, they are required to notify you about the changes.

Often times, especially with the annual copy, the notice is included as an insert with your monthly bill or at any other time, you may receive it as a separate mail item. Make sure you take the time to read these policies in their entirety so you have a clear understanding of how that company is going to handle your personal information. Do not be afraid to get answers to any questions you may have and if necessary, check out various financial institutions to find the one with the privacy policy that best suits your needs.

Each and every time you need to provide any kind of personal information to a business, to include your home address and telephone number, you should request a copy of their privacy policy and inquire about what they do with your information once they have it. We recommend you start doing this with any new business relationship you may establish and if you have not done so already at this point in time, you should obtain the privacy policy of the financial institutions you currently have accounts with.

If within the privacy policy of any new accounts you establish you are given opt-out choices, you need to follow the instructions provided to exercise those options. For any of your existing accounts, if you have not already done so, you need to exercise those options at this time. We will go into more detail about this in future chapters and will provide a check list at the end of the book that will help walk you through this process with your financial institutions.

What Information do Businesses Release?

The type of information a business or company will release depends on that individual company or business. Some businesses may not have a need to share our information, other than what is permitted by law, for them to be able to complete their day to day business objectives. In this case, we will not have the right to any opt-out options. Most other companies as part of their day to day activities will share, sell or release the personal information they have in their customers' files. In this situation, we recommend you exercise all opt-out options that are available to you.

As you conduct your day to day business, you need to keep in mind that there are businesses and companies that will release your personal information to include your home address, home phone number, date of birth and social security number. We, as consumers, need to start asking the necessary questions to get this practice stopped and follow through with what ever opt-out procedure is provided to us so these companies and businesses do not continue to share, sell or release our personal information. Along with releasing our personal identifying information, these companies and businesses also share to similar type businesses our spending habits and where we like to shop. This is a good example of the never ending information sharing cycle and why we receive so many credit offers and so much junk mail.

Why is it Legal for Businesses to Release our Information?

Basically, there are two federal laws that allow companies involved in financial type activities to release our personal information. The first one is the Fair Credit Reporting Act which deals with the information the credit bureaus are allowed to share. The credit bureaus can only release our information to a third party providing they have shown a reason that is permitted by law. Some examples of an acceptable reason would be to evaluate a credit application, your eligibility or suitability for insurance, or for employment.

Often times, after a business or company obtains your credit report, they will want to share it with one or more of their affiliates. According to the Fair Credit Reporting Act, if the business or company wants to share your information at this point, they should notify you about their intent and give you the option to opt-out to prevent them from doing so. This type of sharing practice and opt-out option is generally included in the privacy policy that you should receive from the company or business that obtained the copy of your credit report.

The second Federal Law that regulates the release of our personal information from financial institutions is the Gramm-Leach-Bliley Act. This is the law that requires business and companies involved with financial type activities to provide us their privacy policies that describe how they handle and share our personal identifying information. One of the main benefits of this Act is that it limits companies and businesses from being able to share our personal information with non-affiliates.

Non-affiliates generally fall within three categories. The first is service providers. These non-affiliates will be other companies hired by your financial institution to perform a specific task or service for your account, i.e. – process your payments, prepare your monthly statement, etc. The second category is joint marketers. The companies and businesses that fall within this group are ones that have an agreement with your financial institution to provide you other products and services. The last category is those companies and businesses described as other third party non-affiliates. This group of non-affiliates will be all those other businesses that want to get a hold of your financial institution's mailing list so they too can offer you other products and services in an attempt to drum up business.

According to the Gramm-Leach-Bliley Act, companies and businesses can share your personal information with non-affiliated service providers and joint marketers, however, before it can share your personal information with other third party non-affiliates, they need to tell you how they share your information and provide you with an option to opt-out from this practice.

We deal with many other companies and businesses in our daily lives that are not involved with financial type activities. There are no specific laws in existence that regulate how all these other types of businesses are suppose to handle or safeguard their customers' personal identifying information. Some companies will take it upon themselves to safeguard their customers' information and provide an opt-out choice. On the other hand, many companies will make it part of their routine business practices to share, sell and release their customers' personal information without affording them an opportunity to not be included in this sharing practice.

As you become aware of the information sharing practices of the businesses you deal with in your daily life, you will start to realize the magnitude of this situation and how prevalent it is for all businesses and companies to share their customers' personal information. These business practices do not seem fair on our part because we would like to think we have a certain expectation of privacy with the companies we choose to deal with in that if we give them our personal information, we intend for it to only be used by that company and not for them to share it with whomever else they wish.

Many businesses will state right in their privacy policies that once we give them our personal identifying information to do business with them they then have the right to share, sell, or release it. Basically, they think they can do whatever they want with it. By agreeing to do business with these companies, we are making our personal information available in publicly available information sources and public record. We need to start asking these companies questions about what we can do to make them stop sharing our personal information.

If you discover you are applying for a credit card with a company that does not have a privacy policy in place that would allow you to opt out of them releasing your information, we recommend that you find a new credit card company that offers you the opportunity of opting out from their sharing practices. There are so many available companies for us to conduct our business with that we do have a choice to select which one we want to give our business to.

As we stated earlier, the most important concept you need to walk away from this book with is that each and every business you deal with will share, sell or release your personal identifying information. Once you understand this, all you need to do is become and remain diligent with asking those questions about how they handle and share your personal information and what you need to do to make them stop.

Like with the public record and publicly available information sources, we have discovered many other sources and methods that are being used to disseminate our personal identifying information. In future chapters, we will discuss these sources and methods in greater detail. At this point, we would like to highlight several other major sources that disseminate our personally identifiable information.

Consumer Credit Reporting Agencies

In the United States, we have four main consumer credit reporting agencies. They are Experian, Equifax, TransUnion, and Innovis. We have all heard of these companies which are more commonly known as the credit bureaus. The main function of these credit bureaus is to compile our credit information which includes our credit and employment histories, financial institutions we have accounts with, our payment history, a list of our creditors for closed and open accounts, and any bankruptcies or lawsuits. They will also track home addresses, phone numbers and other individuals we apply for credit with. When we fill out a credit application and include all our personal information on the application, the involved financial institution will give this information to the credit bureaus.

The credit bureaus are regulated by federal law in how they handle and share our information. As consumers, it is extremely important for each of us to check our credit reports at least once a year. It is our responsibility to know what is in our credit reports and to monitor them to ensure the accuracy of the information that is being reported and collected. If we suspect there are any errors, it is our responsibility to take the initiative to get them corrected. Because the credit bureaus play a major role in the release of our personal identifying information, we will discuss our credit reports in greater detail in later chapters.

Mailing Lists

In completing research on the topic of mailing lists, it is hard to come up with a number of exactly how many businesses are in existence that compiles our information. Creating mailing lists from customer databases is such a huge business in the United States. We, as consumers, can not completely stop our information from being included in these lists, however, there are things that we can do to prevent the release of it to a certain degree.

We went to the Internet and typed in "mailing lists" in the search engine www.google.com. The second hit that came back was for a company that directs you on how to go about buying your own mailing list. Sharing customer information is a very lucrative business and companies are making a lot of money selling our personal information to other companies that want it and who are willing to pay the price.

Companies will collect information based on our spending habits, demographics, postal codes, age, income, life style, hobbies, and homeowner status. After they collect this information, they will turn around and sell it to other companies that want to use it to market their products or services. The businesses that buy the information will generally make contact with us, the consumers, either by sending us an advertisement in the mail or by making phone calls in an attempt to promote their business.

Consumer Marketing Data

The same information that is gathered for creating mailing lists can also be used for consumer marketing data collection. The difference between these two activities is their purpose. Mailing lists are generally used by companies to advertise their products or services whereas the consumer marketing data is used by companies for new product marketing.

Another item also collected by companies is information on our spending habits. Every time you make a purchase utilizing a credit card, certain information surrounding that purchase is gathered to include what you bought, how much you spent, how you paid for it, and where you made the purchase. The companies gathering this information will use it to help identify consumer groups they can target for new product marketing and advertisement.

CHAPTER 3: WHO SELLS OUR PERSONAL INFORMATION?

This chapter will help us identify our creditors and those businesses and companies we deal with on a regular basis in our daily lives. To prepare for future chapters, we are going to have you start creating a list of all your creditors and all those businesses you deal with on a regular basis that have your personal identifying information.

As you go day to day conducting your personal business, identify each and every company and business you deal with on a daily, weekly, monthly and/or annual basis. Start writing these business names in a journal. The entities that should definitely be included in this list are the companies and businesses that have any item of your personal information such as your name, date of birth, social security number, home address, and home phone number. Make sure you write down the business name and exactly what specific personal identifying information they have on you.

By creating this list early on, it will make the later steps of the protection process easier. When you get into the action mode of protecting your personal information, you will have a head start since you will have already started compiling your list.

Businesses and Companies

In the previous chapters, we talked about some of the types of businesses and companies that sell our information, i.e. - credit bureaus, mailing lists and consumer marketing data companies. The businesses and companies at this higher level are the ones that buy and collect information from the smaller businesses that we deal with directly to do our business. To better understand the difference between the levels of these businesses, we have included the diagram below to help illustrate these relationships.

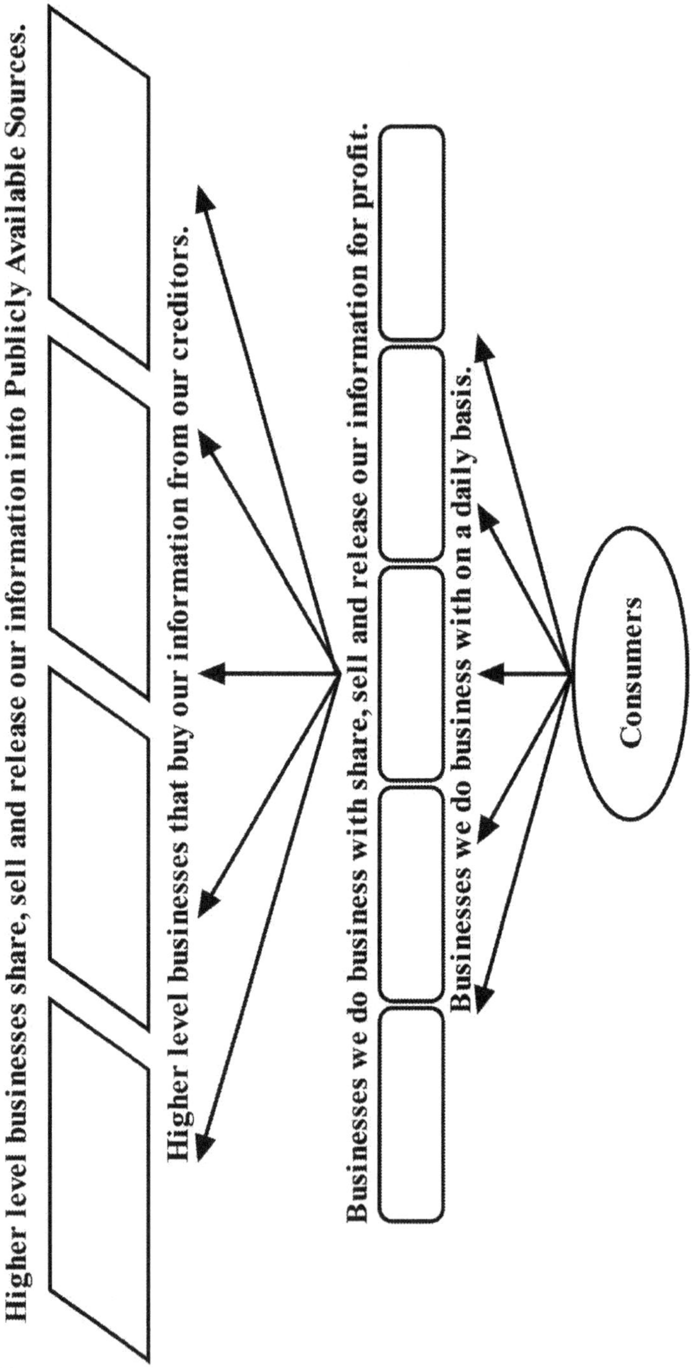
Higher level businesses share, sell and release our information into Publicly Available Sources.
Higher level businesses that buy our information from our creditors.
Businesses we do business with share, sell and release our information for profit.
Businesses we do business with on a daily basis.
Consumers

We do not directly give these higher level businesses our personal identifying information. Our information is generally gathered by the lower level businesses we interact with on a regular basis. Let us talk in more detail about the businesses and companies we deal with on a daily business that share, sell and release our personal information.

Businesses and companies need our personal information to provide us, the customer, with the specific service they offer. We give the business our information in good faith believing the information we provide them is meant only so they can provide us a service. We do not realize that these businesses, in a majority of cases, turn around and share, sell or release our information to higher level businesses, usually to make a profit.

To assist us with understanding this concept, as we progress through the chapters, we need to take a look at what we do on a daily basis in our personal lives and identify what companies and businesses we have a relationship with. Each person's life style is different so we do not have one model that fits each and every person that reads this book. You will need to take a look at your life to identify the specific businesses you have contact with on a daily, weekly, monthly and\or annual basis. You will need to determine what personal information they have on you, become familiar with their privacy policy, and exercise any and all opt-out options they provide. We can not stress to you enough that these businesses and companies are making more money selling your personal information than they are just having you as a customer.

Throughout this book, we will discuss numerous examples of the types of businesses you may deal with that are releasing your information. The main idea we want to stress in this section is getting you to understand that when we, as consumers, give a company or business our personal identifying information that business will probably share, sell or release it to a higher level business that in turn compiles and re-sells it to publicly available information sources.

Some examples of the types of businesses we deal with on a regular basis that are sharing our personally identifiable information are:

Newspapers

Movie rentals stores

Grocery store discount cards

Department stores

Gas Stations

Restaurants

For your convenience, we have included a form that will assist you with creating your list of the businesses and companies you deal with on a regular basis. You should be most interested in those businesses that have any item of your personally identifiable information, such as your name, date of birth, social security number, home address and home phone number. Keep the journal with you and start compiling this information. This task may take you awhile, because you may not realize initially how many business relationships you actually have. Be patient and diligent and have the confidence that it will all come together at the end of the protection process.

List of Businesses

List of businesses you do business with on a daily, weekly and monthly basis.

Your Creditors

Our creditors are heavily involved with sharing, selling and releasing our personal identifying information for profit. Like the businesses and companies we deal with, we all have different credit backgrounds so we will all have different creditors that we deal with. For right now, let us talk about who some of your creditors might be. Each and every business you receive monthly statements from, businesses you make payments to each month, and all those businesses that you have accounts with that show "open" on your credit reports are considered your creditors.

We want you to start identifying all your creditors and create a list utilizing the form below. If you start creating this list now and add to it as we move through the chapters, it will make the protection process easier for you to complete.

This form is also available as a MS Word document on our website, www.personalinfoprotection.com, if you prefer to work with an electronic copy.

List of Creditors

Credit Cards
(department store, furniture)

____
____
____
____
____

Magazines

____
____
____
____
____

Mortgage Loans
(home equity, second, mortgage)

____
____
____
____
____

Vehicle Loans

____
____
____
____
____

Phone
(home, cell, pager)

____
____
____
____
____

Utility
(electric, water, garbage, gas, HOA’s)

____
____
____
____
____

TV/Internet
(cable, satellite, internet service provider)

____
____
____
____
____
____

Insurance Company's
(home, vehicle, life, health, dental)

____
____
____
____
____
____

Misc Loans or bills
(student loans, ect.)

____
____
____
____
____
____

Memberships
(gym, professional, church, hobbies)

____
____
____
____
____
____

PART II: PREVENTION TECHNIQUES

Introduction

In this section, we will begin talking about the action steps you must take to start the process of protecting your personal information. We call it a process because it will take you some time to get all the required information together to be able to initiate each step we recommend after which there will be some maintenance involved to ensure the integrity of your protected information. As you go through this process, you will learn how your personal information gets into public record and other publicly available information sources like the ones we discussed in Part I.

After you gain this understanding of how, it will then be easy to recognize what you need to do to protect yourself by preventing your personal information from being shared, sold and released as you proceed with your day to day financial and business activities. At the point in time when you complete the set-up portion of this process, you can not just continue living your life and forget about what you have done and why. You must be diligent each and every day to ensure your personal information will not be shared, sold or released by the companies and businesses you deal with in your daily life.

CHAPTER 4: GET A PRIVATE PO BOX

One of the most important pieces of your personal information that needs to be protected is your home address. Because we are trying to protect this information, we need to look at some options that will help us accomplish this. The very first step we recommend you take to begin the process of protecting your personal information is obtain a mailing address you can start using in place of your residence address. Two options we have identified that we need to discuss are the different types of alternate addresses that are available for us to use in place of our home address.

PO Box from the United States Postal Service

One type of available address is a PO Box obtained from a U.S. Post Office. We do not recommend getting this type of address unless it is as an absolute last resort. This address when written out, PO Box 1234, indicates to anyone looking at it that it represents a post office box. You can only use this type of post office box to receive mail, such as letters and bills. The Post Office will not accept packages for you if they are sent to this type of address.

We are sure many of you may already be using a PO Box from the Post Office as an address. If you are, you will need to decide whether or not you are going to make a change after we explain another viable option. If you choose not to change from using a PO Box type address, at least you have it set up already that you are receiving your mail at your PO Box instead of at your residence. At this point in the process, just make sure all your mail is in fact being sent to your PO Box and you are receiving no type of mail at your physical residence.

Private PO Box

Another type of available address is a mailbox obtained from a private business. A private PO Box will generally have a mailing address that looks like a regular street address and the box number will look like an apartment number, similar to 1234 West Grand Avenue #107161. This is the type of address we strongly recommend and encourage you to get because the address does look like an apartment address and is not easily recognizable as a PO Box.

When you start looking for these private mailbox businesses, you will find them everywhere. The businesses are all privately owned and will usually conduct mailing, copying, and other miscellaneous mail-type services. These privately owned post office businesses are becoming very popular and are starting to show up in a variety of locations.

Once you identify the privately owned mailing-type business that is conveniently located to fit your lifestyle, you will need to go in and make contact with the owner. We recommend you bypass all the employees and go straight to the business owner because you will need to ask them questions about how they operate their business and how they are going to protect your information. The regular employees may not have the answers to the specific questions you will be asking. Make sure you develop a relationship with the business owner as you will need to be able to count on that owner to help protect your personal information.

When you fill out the application to obtain a private mail box, you will need to provide such information as your home address and a copy of your driver license. Ask the owner what they do with your personal information once it has been provided. Specifically ask if they just throw the information in a box that is kept under the front counter, do they lock the information in the office, or do they keep it in a safe? You should also specifically ask the owner if they share, sell or release your personal information to third parties. The owner needs to know how important it is to you that they protect your personal information. Go with your gut instinct if you decide to get a mailbox with any particular privately owned business. If it does not feel right after talking with the owner, take your business elsewhere.

Another advantage to utilizing a private mailbox is that most of these privately owned businesses will accept packages on behalf of their customers. Make sure you specifically ask the owner this question too. It is important to find a mailing business that does accept packages for their customers as this will eliminate the need to have any packages sent to your home address.

Stop Using Your Home Address

Once you have established a private mailbox, you will need to stop using your home address to receive mail and packages. Your home address needs to stop existing on paper and you need to stop using it period. You will need to make the necessary arrangements so that all your mail and packages are sent to your private mailbox and not to your home address. In future chapters, we will walk you through how to make these necessary arrangements and who you need to contact.

At this point in the process, it is important to know that you need to make it look like you are moving on paper from your residence to your new private mailing address. Go to the post office and fill out change of address cards indicating you are moving from your home to your private mailbox. This is an excellent way to make it look like you are moving on paper. The U.S. Post Office views change of address cards as public record and will share this information under limited circumstances so this is a good step to complete to really make it look like you are moving.

We also recommend that once you have your private mailbox established, you start using your private mailing address like it is your home address and stop putting your home address down on credit applications. Since your private mailbox address looks like an apartment, most creditors will not recognize the fact that it is not a residential address.

If you have the traditional PO Box through the U.S. Post Office, you may have problems using it as your home address on credit applications as it is easily recognizable as a post office box and not a residence. This is one of the main reasons why we recommend obtaining a private mailbox instead of a PO Box through the U.S. Post Office. If you do not use a lot of credit and can get away with the traditional PO Box then this type of address is an acceptable alternative.

Because you are trying to protect your home address, you also need to understand that you can not have any packages for you or your family members mailed to your residence. If you choose to utilize a traditional PO Box, this is one obstacle you will need to over come. The U.S. Post Office will not accept packages for their customers so you will need to come up with an alternate way to receive packages other than using your home address. In a later chapter, we will discuss another compelling reason why you do not want packages sent to your residence address.

CHAPTER 5: IDENTIFY A DESIGNATED PHONE NUMBER

Another piece of our personal information that we need to protect is our home telephone number. With technology advancements and the increasing demands that have been placed on our lives, we moved quickly into the days of having multiple phone numbers being used per person. It is not uncommon for each of us to have a home, cell, pager and work number. We need to talk about these different types of phone numbers and how we can best utilize each number we have to further protect ourselves and our families.

Home Phone

Our home telephone number is probably the longest standing phone number we may still have. We are, however, seeing a future where many of us will no longer use a home telephone. We are aware of an increasing number of individuals who already do not have a home phone and are just utilizing a cell phone.

Because your home telephone phone number is directly linked to your residence address, we need to specifically discuss this number. We definitely recommend you pay the extra charges through your service provider to have your home phone number non-published and non-listed. By doing this, you are preventing your service provider from being able to share, sell or release your personal information into any type of directory or phone listing. The personal information that is included in these telephone directories and is subject to release is our name, home address, and home telephone number. Telephone directories are one of the major sources of personal information collected by the Internet databases

You need to be very selective with who you give your home telephone number to. It is okay for your family and friends to have this number; however, we do not recommend you give out your home telephone number under any other circumstances. If you have reviewed your creditors' opt-out policies and have your accounts tagged to not share, sell or release, only under these limited circumstances, would we recommend you consider allowing your creditors to have your home telephone number. Our first preference and what we strongly encourage you to do is not give your home telephone number to any of your creditors.

Even though your home telephone number is unpublished and unlisted, you will still receive random telemarketing calls. You can not completely prevent this from happening but you can reduce the frequency with which it occurs. We recommend you place your home telephone number on the "do not call" registry at www.donotcall.gov or by calling 1-888-382-1222. Keep in mind this registry is not a cure all for stopping telemarketing calls but it is a great place to start. This national "do not call" registry is managed by the Federal Trade Commission. If you are interested in learning more about this topic, the Federal Trade Commission's website contains a wealth of information on this subject matter.

We also recommend you do not put your home telephone number down on any credit applications as this is one personal information item that they will share, sell and release. When you fill out a credit application, you are providing that company with your personal identifying information, which will then be considered publicly available information.

As you will learn in this book, you need to ask the companies and businesses you deal with those questions about what they do with your personal information and what their opt-out policies are before even filling out the credit application. You need to be diligent in asking these questions and providing information such as your private mailbox address instead of your home address and a telephone number other than your home number. If you can not control the company from releasing your information at least you can control what information they have to release.

As we stated previously, we do not recommend you give out your home telephone number as it is linked to your home address. Even with your diligence in asking all the right questions and electing all the available opt-out choices, your personal information may still get out into publicly available information sources.

Cell Phone

The day is here when most people have a cell phone and it is getting to the point where this is the only number a majority of us are using. Cell phone usage is more prevalent in the larger cities than it is in the rural areas. Cell coverage has a tendency to be weaker in these more remote locations. It will not take long for this to change as technology continues to advance in leaps and bounds. We do see a time in the very near future when the only phone number people will elect to use will be their cell phone numbers.

We realize that for years the e-mails and rumors have gone around that our cell phone service providers are sharing, selling and releasing our personal information. At the time this book goes to publication, there is no truth to these rumors. Since law enforcement still needs to obtain a subpoena to get cell phone subscriber information, we are fairly certain this rumor is not true. There will be a day when it will be a fact and we need to keep up with this so we will be able to protect our information before it is released. Our cell phone providers will probably notify us that this is going to occur and provide us with an opportunity to opt-out from this happening. We will eventually have to start paying those extra charges for non-published and non-listed numbers just like our home phones.

Until we do see a change with our cell phone providers, your cell phone number is a great number to give out to your creditors and to put on credit applications. As with your home phone, be very selective with whom you give this information out to. We suggest you use the rule of thumb that if you want a phone call back from the business you are dealing with then give them your cell phone number. Even if you are going to give your cell phone number out, you still need to be diligent with asking the question if they share, sell or release this information and if they do, make sure you have them tag your account so they do not do so. At the time you sit down to fill out a credit application, ask the question if your information is sold and find out what you need to do to stop this particular business from doing so. If the business gives you opt-out choices so they do not share, sell or release your information then put your cell phone number on the credit application. Even though the personal information maintained by our cell phone provider is a bit more protected, we still need to ask those important questions about whether they share, sell or release our information to their affiliates and non-affiliates.

Pager

Pagers are not as popular as they once were five or ten years ago, but many of us still carry them. If you are required to keep a pager or are in a position to maintain one, feel free to do so. Your pager number is an ideal number to give out to creditors who you do not want a phone call back from. Better yet, if you have voice mail on your pager, we recommend you put your pager number down on your credit applications and give it to all your creditors instead of your cell phone or home telephone number. The business can call, leave a message, and you can place a return call at your convenience. If you do not have a pager, we do not necessarily recommend you go get one as long as you are exercising your opt-out options with your creditors and you have a cell phone number to provide them.

Work Phone

Most of us have phone numbers where we can be contacted while we are at work. Depending on what line of work you are in, you need to decide if your work number is the best phone number to give to your creditors. We do not recommend you give this phone number to your creditors or provide it on credit applications. You are the best person to evaluate your own particular situation and make the decision that best suits your needs.

Designated Phone Number

We have discussed several different types of phone numbers you may utilize in your daily life. We recommend you select one as your designated phone number to give to your creditors and put on credit applications. If you are going to use a pager as your designated phone number, this will work out great for those creditors you do not want a phone call back from. If you are not going to use a pager number, your next option would be to use your cell phone number. When you give your cell phone number to these businesses you may not want a phone call back from, let that business know you do not want to receive any kind of telemarketing calls. Make sure you tell them right from the get go to tag your account that you do not want to receive any phone calls from them unless it has something specifically to do with your account.

Why is it so important for us to talk about what type of phone numbers you have? The bottom line is you are trying to protect your home address. Your home phone number is tied directly to your home address so we do not recommend you give your home number out at all and if you absolutely have to, give it out sparingly. Your cell phone and pager numbers are great numbers to give to your creditors because you will have these accounts set up so they do not come back to your home address. We will talk about how to do this in a future chapter.

The ideal goal we are trying to accomplish in this book is protecting your home address and anything linked to it from getting into public record and publicly available information sources. Since your home telephone number is linked to your home address, have a plan of action ready on what phone number you are going to provide when a business, company, or creditor asks you for one during your day to day transactions.

We have several examples to further illustrate what we have talked about in previous chapters:

1.) You are buying a new vehicle and while filling out the credit application at the dealership, you are asking the questions about whether they share, sell or release your personal information. Since to some extent they are going to share your personal information, we recommend you give them your private PO Box as if it is your home address and whatever phone number you have chosen as your designated number. You will receive phone calls from the dealership, which is why you want to provide them with an alternate phone number like a pager so they can not directly contact you. When using your private PO Box like it is your home address, do not let the creditor know it is a mailing address. Remember, on paper you need to make it look as if you are living at your private PO Box. If you have a post office box through the U.S. Postal Service, it will look like a PO Box and the creditor will know it is not your physical address. The dealership may reject your credit application with the PO Box on it, at which time, you will need to provide your true home address otherwise you may not be approved for the financing necessary to purchase the vehicle you want to buy. This is the main reason why you want the private mailing address because it looks like an apartment and it will not raise any red flags that it is not your physical home address as it is not easily recognizable as a PO Box.

2.) You are applying for new credit, such as a credit card. There is no reason why these companies need your home address and home phone number. When completing these types of applications, use your private PO Box like it is your home address and provide your designated phone number (pager or cell phone number). During the application process, make sure you are exercising your opt-out choices and have the company tag your account right from the beginning to not share, sell or release your personal identifying information.

CHAPTER 6: CONTACT YOUR CREDITORS

In this chapter, we will be using the list you have been working on since Chapter 3. If you have not completed your list yet, continue to take the time to get it filled out. Completing this list will make the steps in this chapter easier as you will have identified a majority of your creditors and the lower level businesses you deal with on a regular basis.

Hopefully, by now, you have also gotten your private PO Box. As we stated previously, establishing your private mailing address is the first step in the protection process along with identifying your designated phone number. The next step you need to complete is contacting every one of your creditors. Your creditors are involved with sharing, selling and releasing your personal information. They are making a lot of money doing this and are definitely a part of that two billion dollar information sharing industry.

Who are Your Creditors?

You need to identify who your creditors are. Your creditors are the businesses you:

1.) Receive statements from monthly, quarterly or yearly.

2.) Pay money to on a regular and routine basis. Make sure you identify all your creditors. You may be paying most of them on a monthly basis but do not forget about those insurance policies you are paying every six months or annually. Go through your check register and files for the past couple of years and identify each and every creditor you have paid money to and who may have any of your personal identifying information.

3.) You will also have creditors listed in your credit report. If you have an account showing "open" on your credit report but are not receiving statements or currently paying money on the account, the business or company is still considered one of your creditors. Make sure you obtain a copy of your credit report and identify all the accounts designated as "open". We will cover credit reports more in-depth later in this chapter and in Chapter 7.

As you identify who your creditors are, continue adding them to your list from Chapter 3. Because you do not deal with all your creditors on a monthly basis, it is going to take some time for you to make your list all inclusive. It is important that you take the time to gather all of this information and then follow the steps we recommend once they have been identified. Depending on your credit background, this part of the process may take longer for some than others. If you are married, make sure your spouse is completing all these steps as well. You are directly linked to your spouse in your credit reports so they also need to be involved as you go through the protection process.

Credit Reports

We recommend you obtain a copy of your credit report from each of the three credit bureaus (Equifax, Experian and TransUnion). We suggest you do this at least once a year, as a minimum, but recommend you do it twice, if possible. As part of the protection process, we want you to get a current copy of your credit reports now so you will be able to identify any accounts designated as "open".

We, as consumers, can get one free credit report per credit bureau per year. You need to take advantage of this opportunity and start making this a routine practice in your personal life if you have not already done so. The website to obtain your free credit reports is www.annualcreditreport.com. This website will link you directly to the three credit bureaus (Experian, Equifax, and TransUnion) so you can order your credit reports. If you do not feel comfortable providing your personal identifying information over the Internet, you can contact the credit bureaus directly by telephone to obtain your credit report copies.

Requesting your own credit report will not reflect negatively on your credit score. It does not count against us when we request our own credit reports. It only counts against us when companies and businesses make inquiries into our credit reports or when we fill out an application to open a new credit account.

Once you have your credit reports in hand, review each report in its entirety for accuracy. Identify each and every account listed, but pay particular attention to those accounts that are showing as "open". All the businesses and companies that you have "open" accounts with are still considered your creditors. You need to write down on your worksheet all the accounts that are showing "open" in your credit report. If you have not had any activity on an "open" account for years, we recommend you consider closing that account. We will talk further about this idea in a later chapter.

Now that we have talked about the three ways to identify who your creditors are, you need to take the time and make sure you have included all of them on your worksheet. The next step in the protection process we are going to cover is you contacting all the creditors you have just identified.

Contacting Your Creditors

This is one of the most important steps in the protection process and it will be one of the most time consuming. Each of our credit backgrounds is different so we will have various numbers and types of creditors to identify. Because we have diverse credit backgrounds, we are unable to provide you with one all inclusive list that everyone can use. Also, because of these varying backgrounds, it is extremely important for you to take the time you need to go through your records and identify every creditor from your past and in the present.

When you have your list of creditors completed, you will need to call each one of them. There are two things you need to accomplish during these contacts.

1.) The first is you need to get your creditors to stop sharing, selling and releasing your personal identifying information. As we have already learned, all of your creditors are selling your information and are making money doing it. Each creditor will have a privacy policy which will include what your opt-out options are. Get on your creditor's website or ask the question to the representative you are dealing with on the phone what it is you need to do to get them to stop selling your personal identifying information. Some creditors will tag your account over the phone, some will require you put your request in writing and send them a letter, and others will have their own form they will mail to you that you need to fill out and mail back to them. Make sure you do whatever it takes with each of your creditors to get them to stop sharing, selling and releasing your personal identifying information.
2.) The second thing you need to do while you have your creditors on the phone is change your address and telephone number so all their correspondence with you will start going to your private mailing address. For address change purposes, you can put your creditors into two different categories:
    a. The first category is those creditors that do not need your true home address. These companies and businesses do not provide any kind of service at your residence so they do not need your real home address. Examples of these types of creditors are credit cards, life insurance policies, magazines, cell phones, pagers, memberships, student loans, vehicle loans, etc. Because these types of businesses do not need your home address, when you have their representative on the phone tagging your account to not share, sell or release

your information, you need to tell them to change the address on your account and give them your private PO Box and new contact or designated phone number. This is one of the main reasons why we recommended you get a private mailing address that looks like an apartment so you can provide it to your creditors as if it is your home address. Your creditors do not need to know that your mailing address is a PO Box and not your home address. Tell them it is your new address and leave it at that. Ensure they make the address and phone number change to your account.

b. The second category of creditor is the one that will need your true home address for service. Some examples of these businesses are mortgage companies, home and vehicle insurance companies, as well as utilities to include electric, gas, phone, cable, etc. These companies and businesses will need your home address for service but have them list your mailing address as the contact (customer) address and request they mail your monthly bills or statements to this mailing address. Creditors in this category will separate the service and customer address and send everything to your private mailing address. Most of your utility companies do not share, sell or release your personal identifying information, but while you have them on the phone ask them about their privacy policies and opt-out options to ensure they are not selling your information. With the service provider that handles your home phone, make sure you pay the extra charges for a non-published and non-listed number. This will ensure your phone company does not share, sell or release your personal identifying information. The businesses in this category that we do know will share your personal information will be the mortgage companies and insurance companies. Make sure you are reviewing their privacy policies and exercising your opt-out options.

At this point in time, you should have made contact with all your creditors from your list. All your accounts should now be tagged so the businesses and companies you have financial dealings with are not sharing, selling or releasing your personal identifying information. Once you accomplish this step in the protection process, you can not just stop here and forget about what you have done. You will need to stay on top of this with each transaction you complete during your day to day activities. You will need to monitor your current creditors and make sure your accounts remain tagged and remember to have your new creditor's tag your accounts from the beginning of the application process so these lower level businesses do not share, sell or release your personal identifying information.

List of Creditors and What to Give Them as Your Contact Information

- Credit Cards – give all your credit card companies your private PO Box as your home address and your cell phone number as your contact number. These creditors will need a viable way to contact you in case they need to notify you for identity theft reasons. Because your credit card companies are a major source for the release of your personal information, make sure they have your accounts tagged to not share, sell or release.
- Magazines – give them your private PO Box as your home address and your designated phone number. You do not want calls from these companies so do not give them your home or cell phone numbers. Most magazine companies will share, sell or release your personal information and they generally do not offer you any opt-out options. The best you can do with this situation is to make sure no magazines are delivered to your

home address by providing your private PO Box as if it is your home address. We have found a few magazines and mail order catalogs that do provide their customers the opportunity to be removed from their mailing lists. To ensure you do not miss out on an opt-out option, we recommend you also ask your magazine and mail order companies if they have a privacy policy and any available opt-out options. Magazines and mail order companies are another main source of how your personal information is getting into the Internet databases and other publicly available information sources.

- Insurance Companies –
    - ✓ Vehicle Insurance Companies – these companies need your home address to provide you insurance, but make sure they have your private PO Box as your mailing address and cell phone number as a contact number. Vehicle insurance companies also share, sell and release your information so when you have them on the phone providing them with your address and phone number change, ask what opt-out options are available to you.
    - ✓ Home Owner's or Renter's Insurance Companies – these types of companies will also need your home address to provide you with insurance. As with your vehicle insurance policy, make sure they have your private PO Box as your mailing address and cell phone number as your contact number. You also need to determine what you need to do so they do not share, sell or release your personal information.
    - ✓ Life Insurance – your life insurance policies are not tied to your home address in any way so the companies that provide you these policies do not need your home address. Make sure they have your private PO Box as your home address and your cell phone number as a contact number. You need to find out what opt-out

options are available to you and you need to ensure you do what is required so they do not share, sell or release your personal identifying information.

- ✓ Health and Dental Insurance Companies – if you get these policies through your employer, these companies will already have your home address and home phone number. We recommend finding out if you can change your home address to your private PO Box and cell phone number as your contact number. If your employer or health insurance company will not let you do this then make sure they designate your private PO Box as your mailing address and request your mail be sent there instead of to your residence. Also ask about the insurance company's privacy policy and exercise any available opt-out options.

➢ Mortgage Loans – make sure all your mortgage loans are listed on your worksheet. Do not forget about any home equity lines of credit, second mortgages or refinancing loans. You will need to contact all of your home mortgage companies as well. These companies will need your home address for your loan purposes, but have them use your private PO Box as your mailing address and give them your cell phone number as a contact number. Ask about their privacy policies and what your opt-out options are so they do not share, sell or release your personal identifying information.

- ✓ Because we know the companies that provide you your mortgage loans share your personal information, you need to ask what they do with your personal information throughout the entire process. There are so many people who get your personal identifying information during the mortgage loan process. You need to let it be known at every step along the way that you do not want your personal information shared, sold or released and do whatever it takes to make sure this does not happen. Getting to your mortgage loan companies is very important with protecting your home information.

- ✓ You also need to remember that when the documents relating to these loans are filed through your state's recorder's office, this information is then considered public record and available for public inspection. As we discussed earlier, many states are making this information available on-line. At this point in time, we are unable to prevent these documents from being filed and considered public record.

- ➢ Vehicle Loans – this is another type of lender that does not need your home address and home phone number. We recommend you do a change of address and provide them your private PO Box as your home address and your cell phone number as your contact number. Make sure you find out what their privacy policy is and do whatever it takes so they do not share, sell or release your personal information.
  - ✓ As with the mortgage loan process, you need to start at the very beginning of the loan process when you are purchasing a new vehicle. Advise whoever you are dealing with every step of the way that you do not want them to share, sell or release your personal identifying information and do what it takes to get them to stop.
- ➢ Memberships – because we are individuals with different interests, the types of organizations and groups we might belong to varies immensely. Some examples of the memberships we are referring to might be the church you belong to, the gym where you work out, any professional groups you might be a member of or a group based on one of your hobbies. These groups and organizations do not need your home address and home phone number. Contact all of the groups you belong to,

whether you are an active participant or not, and change the address they have on file for you to your private PO Box and your contact number to your cell phone number. Many of these organizations will not have privacy policies and opt-out options so there is a good chance your personal information could find its way into a publicly available information source or an Internet database.

A good example that demonstrates this point is a church membership directory. The church may not sell this list, but they put the information into a directory and pass it out to all the congregation members. Once the list makes it into the hands of the members, we can not control what those members do with it, however, we can control what information is put into the directory in the first place. So your home address does not get into the wrong hands in this situation, make sure you only provide your private mailing address and cell phone number. Most organizations provide directory lists to their members, which works great for making the group's members accessible to each other. Just be wary of this and control what information is put into these types of directories.

- Phone Companies
    - ✓ Home phone – this company needs your home address for service, but provide them with your private PO Box as your mailing address and ensure this is the address where they will send you your bills. It is also extremely important to pay those extra charges for a non-published, non-listed number so your phone company does not share, sell or release your personal information. Phone directories are considered a publicly available information source and are major contributors to the information that is released into the Internet databases.
    - ✓ Cell phone Providers – there is no need for this account to be tied to your home address. Use your private

PO Box as your home address. At the time this book goes to publication, the cell phone companies are not sharing, selling or releasing your personal information. We foresee this changing at some point in the near future so we recommend you closely monitor your service provider's privacy policy and make sure when this does happen you take the necessary steps to prevent the release of your personal information.

- ✓ Pager companies – these service providers are very similar to the cell phone companies. There is no reason why they need your home address so provide them your private PO Box as if it is your home address. If you are going to maintain a personal pager, make sure you ask about the service provider's privacy policy and exercise any necessary opt-out options. We also foresee a time in the future when pagers will no longer exist and everyone will be using cell phones.

- ➢ Utility companies – we are going to group all these companies together. Your utility companies will need your home address to provide you service, but make sure you give them your private PO Box as your mailing address and your cell phone number as a contact number. Even though most of the utility companies are not sharing their customers' information, you still need to be familiar with their privacy policies. Ask the question if they share, sell or release and find out if any opt-out options are available.
- ➢ TV/Cable/Internet Service Providers – these types of companies will also need your home address for service. Provide them with your private PO Box as your mailing address and cell phone number as a contact number. Ensure all the bills go to your mailing address. It is also important to ask these companies what their privacy policies are and do what it takes

so they do not share, sell or release your personal identifying information.

- Miscellaneous Loans – this is another area that will be different for each of us. You need to take a close look at your credit background. Use the list you created in Chapter 3 and make sure you contact all the creditors you identified that we have not mentioned. Ask the questions about their privacy policies and complete the available opt-out options so they do not share, sell or release your personal information.
  - ✓ If any of these businesses or companies need your home address for service, make sure you provide them your private PO Box as your mailing address.
  - ✓ If there is no reason for the company or business to have your home address then do a change of address with them and use your private PO Box as if it is your home address.

CHAPTER 7: THE CREDIT BUREAUS AND YOUR CREDIT REPORT

In this day and age of identity theft and the emphasis that is placed on the importance of our credit reports, it is amazing that many of us do not check our credit reports to see what is contained in them. It is a common business practice that our credit reports are queried for a variety of reasons. We can not even get a line of credit from a lower level business without having them check our credit report. Our current creditors also check our credit reports periodically to ensure we are maintaining our creditworthiness. The businesses and companies we deal with in our daily financial activities check our credit reports, yet so many of us have never looked at a copy of our report much less have any idea what information is in them. This is a major oversight on our part and is one area where we need to change our way of thinking and take action.

Check Your Credit Report Yearly

We recommend you check your credit reports at least once a year, preferably twice. You are ultimately responsible for what is in your credit report; be in control of your own credit report and what is found within its pages. All three credit bureaus will provide you with information on how to read and understand your credit report so do not hesitate to turn to them for assistance with any questions you may have.

There are several ways to obtain your credit report.

1. The first way is through the website www.annualcreditreport.com. This is the website where you can get all three of your credit reports. You are allowed to get one free credit report per credit bureau per year. When you access this website, they will

ask you for personal information to verify you are who you say you are.

2. The second way to get your credit reports is directly from each credit bureau.
    a. TransUnion – www.transunion.com
       1-800-888-4213
       PO Box 1000, Chester, PA 19022
    b. Equifax – www.equifax.com
       1-800-685-1111
       PO Box 740241 Atlanta, GA 30374-0241
    c. Experian – www.experian.com
       1-888-397-3742
       PO Box 2002 Allen, TX 75013

Now that you have copies of your credit reports and are learning about the different accounts listed, pay particular attention to which accounts are "open" and which ones are "closed". When you get your credit reports, make sure you have the credit bureaus also provide you with information on how to read and understand them.

Open Accounts

"Open" accounts are the companies and businesses that are considered your current creditors. We talked about the different types of creditors back in Chapter 6. We recommend you control what accounts are "open" and "closed" on your credit reports. Take a good long look at what accounts show as "open" on your credit reports and review the information for accuracy. Identify each account and know what they are.

If you have several "open" accounts on your credit reports but no longer use this particular line of credit or do not have the credit cards for these accounts, you may want to consider closing them. If you have several of these types of "open" accounts and the identity thieves were able to get your credit report, they could re-order these credit cards and go shopping. You would not even know this was occurring until that creditor started contacting you about late payments.

If you identify several accounts you want to close, we recommend you close these accounts at a time when you will not need your credit. Do not close the accounts right before you want to make a major purchase such as a house or a vehicle. Initially, when you close these accounts, your credit score will go down temporarily but it will go right back up after a few months. For this reason, we recommend you close these accounts at a time when you do not need your credit.

There are two ways to close these types of accounts. We recommend you do both.

1. The first way is to contact the creditor directly. The business or company will need to close your account in their system. This creditor will solicit you with offers in an attempt to get you to keep your account "open" so make sure closing the account is really what you want to do.
2. The second way is by contacting the credit bureaus. We recommend writing letters to all the credit bureaus. In your letters, provide a list of all the creditors to include addresses and account numbers, explain that you wish to close these accounts and have them shown on your credit report as "closed". The credit bureaus are great at taking care of this and will usually do so within 30 days after which they will notify you in writing when it is done.

Closed Accounts

As you look at your credit reports, you will also see all the "closed" accounts. These "closed" accounts will not come off your credit report for either seven or ten years depending on what type of account it is. We do not have any control over this. If you have some blemishes on your credit, it will take that long to get them off.

The credit bureaus will also allow you to add an explanation to your credit reports about these blemished "closed" accounts. If you choose to provide an explanation, write a letter to the credit bureaus, put a separate section in your letter explaining each of these accounts and what wording you want listed in your reports about these particular accounts. If you are closing accounts, you can provide your explanation in the same letter just make sure you write separate sections explaining each and what you wish to accomplish on your credit report.

Questions Asked on Credit Applications

Next, we need to have an understanding of the actual credit applications we fill out. Back in Chapter 1, we talked about what is considered public record and publicly available information. When we provide a lower level business our name, home address, home phone number, date of birth and social security number they then consider these items publicly available information and will share, sell or release that information. This is the reason why we need to find out what the businesses and companies we provide our personal information to do with it right from the beginning and get this practice stopped before it has a chance to get started.

Another block on credit applications that is considered publicly available information and sold is the block that asks you to list a relative not living with you. You will be linked directly to those you put down in this block and also to those who put you down. There are several Internet databases that will do these links utilizing this particular block from credit applications. We can not avoid putting someone's information in this block. We recommend you be selective with whom you choose to list. If you have a family member that has a private PO Box, they would be a good choice to use here. We also recommend you find out who in your family is listing you in this block when they fill out credit applications. If they absolutely have to put your information in this block, make sure they are using your private

PO Box and designated phone number rather than your home address and home phone number.

Credit Bureaus are Selling our Personal Identifying Information

As much as you need to monitor your credit reports and make sure they are accurate in what is reported on them, you also need to understand that the credit bureaus will share, sell and release your personal identifying information. The items usually released are your name, home address, home phone number, date of birth and social security number. These items are considered publicly available information.

We need to get to the credit bureaus, utilizing their opt-out rules, to stop this part of the information sharing cycle. Several of the Internet databases will purchase our personal information from the credit bureaus on a regular basis. There are several things you need to do to get the credit bureaus to stop sharing, selling and releasing your personal information.

1. The first thing you need to do is contact all the credit bureaus and permanently opt-out from them releasing your information. You have to make this request in writing. At the end of this chapter, we have included some sample letters for your use. You need to write one letter per person per credit bureau. If you are a female and have had several different last names, make sure you include all those names in your opt-out request letter.
2. The next thing you need to do is get onto www.optoutprescreen.com and go through the steps to permanently opt-out of receiving pre-screened offers of credit and insurance. Once you provide the information requested, a letter will be generated that you need to print off the computer, sign and send in for your request to be permanent. This will stop all the

Consumer Credit Reporting Companies and the credit bureaus from sharing, selling or releasing your personal identifying information for pre-approved / pre-screened offers.

3. Another thing you need to do is go to the Direct Marketing Association's website and do a permanent opt-out through them. Go to www.the-dma.org. Within the privacy policy for consumers, you will find three options that will allow you to remove your home address, home phone number and e-mail address from consumer lists utilized by businesses and companies for marketing purposes.

Credit Bureau Opt-Out Letters

Permanent Opt-Out

<DATE>

Equifax Credit Information Services, Inc
PO Box 740241
Atlanta GA 30374

Re: Name Removal Option

I am writing this letter and providing you with my information to have my name removed to stop prescreened credit and insurance offers. I am also requesting my name, address, phone number to not be shared, sold or released under any circumstances.

First name:
Middle name:
Last names:
Address:
SSN:
DOB:

Thank you for your time and assistance. Please send a letter of confirmation.

<Your Name>
<Your Address>

Permanent Opt-Out

<DATE>

Experian Consumer Services
901 West Bond Street
Lincoln NE 68521

Re: Name Removal Option

I am writing this letter and providing you with my information to have my name removed to stop prescreened credit and insurance offers. I am also requesting my name, address, phone number to not be shared, sold or released under any circumstances.

First name:
Middle name:
Last names:
Address:
Phone:
SSN:
DOB:

Thank you for your time and assistance. Please send a letter of confirmation.

<Your Name>
<Your Address>

Permanent Opt-Out

<DATE>

TransUnion Name Removal Option
PO Box 505
Woodlyn, PA 19094

Re: Name Removal Option

I am writing this letter and providing you with my information to have my name removed to stop prescreened credit and insurance offers. I am also requesting my name, address, phone number to not be shared, sold or released under any circumstances.

First name:
Middle name:
Last names:
Address:
Phone:
SSN:
DOB:

Thank you for your time and assistance. Please send a letter of confirmation.

<Your Name>
<Your Address>

CHAPTER 8: KNOWLEDGE IS POWER!

Knowledge is power. We must gain an understanding of what is going on within the world of public record. Once you start the protection process and start asking your creditors specific questions then you are well on your way to getting the lower level businesses to stop sharing, selling and releasing your personal identifying information. This is a process that needs to start becoming your way of life within every aspect of your financial and business activities. Completing the protection process in the beginning will take some time, but the challenge is to keep it going so you will not have to repeat any of the steps.

Knowing Who Sells Your Personal Information

Keep in mind that every business you come in contact with will inevitably share, sell or release your personal information. These businesses will either do it at the lower level or at the upper corporate level. No matter what you are doing in your daily financial activities those businesses you have a relationship with will share, sell or release your information. Now that you know this and have taken steps to protect your personal identifying information, you will need to stay on top of this and make sure you do what it takes to keep your information protected.

We, as consumers, may need to start being more selective with whom we do business with and take our business to other lower level businesses that allow us to opt-out of them sharing, selling or releasing our personal identifying information. We, as the consumer, have this choice. Maybe it is time for us to take a stand and exercise our freedom of choice. If enough of us start taking a stance, maybe these lower level businesses will start recognizing the consumer's rights not to have their personal information shared unless the business receives the consumer's specific consent. We recognize that laws at the state and federal level need to change but we also know this type of change does not happen over night. The best way we can have an affect on this situation in our own personal lives is to take a stand and make those choices with whom we do business with.

Understanding What You Can Do

Understanding what is going on is the most important step. We may not know everything about what is taking place in regards to the sharing of our personal identifying information, but at the time this book is published, we have researched and tried to understand as much as possible. This endeavor has been and continues to be a learning process, even for us. We learn something new about this information sharing industry every day.

Another thing we need to understand is if we can not completely stop this information sharing practice and the lower level businesses continue sharing, selling and releasing our personal identifying information then we can at least control what information is being released into public record and publicly available information sources. If we know our information is going to be shared, we can control what information is released by providing our private PO Box instead of our home address and our designated phone number instead of our home phone number.

This book is not a cure all for completely stopping the release of your personal identifying information. Use this book as a knowledge base or foundation for understanding what is taking place in the public record world and the role the Internet is playing. This is a problem that is not going to go away and will inevitably get worse as time goes on. Look at how out of control the Internet is right now, it will only get worse in the years to come.

We do not know if we will ever be able to completely stop this information sharing practice. We are certain that there are ways our personal information will continue to get released but we have not yet come across those ways. We are taking our own advice and have completed all the steps in the protection process. So far, what we have done seems to be working.

Because every person's credit back ground is different; you as the reader of this book, may do something completely different in your credit life then we do in ours that will get your personal information shared, sold or released. The main idea we want to stress in this book is that to protect your personal identifying information from being released, you have to make the extra effort and ask those questions to the businesses and companies you deal with to find out what options are available to get this stopped. Hence, trying to understanding what is taking place within this information sharing industry and using the Chapter titled Knowledge is Power as your guide.

Questions to Ask Your Creditors - Current and New

This section pertains to the creditors you currently have and to those you may potentially have. As we previously discussed, no matter what you are doing in your credit world make sure you get to the creditors you already have. From this point forward, get them to stop sharing, selling and releasing your personal identifying information. Change your address to your private PO Box and your phone number to your designated phone number.

Once you have contacted and updated your current creditors, you need to know how to handle any new creditors you may obtain. You need to conduct your daily financial and business activities armed with all the information contained in this book. No matter what you are doing in your credit life you need to understand the business practices of current and new creditors and take the necessary steps to protect your personal information.

Every Day Lower Level Businesses

Now that we have discussed your creditors, we next need to spend some time talking about the lower level businesses you deal with on a daily basis. You should have started compiling a list of these businesses when we provided you the form back in Chapter 3. This form was designed for you to start recognizing all the businesses and companies you deal with on a routine basis, but not necessarily have a line of credit through.

These businesses and companies may also ask you for personal identifying information. Even though you may not have credit through them, they still store information about you as a consumer. As we have mentioned many times previously and want to reiterate here, keep in mind there are businesses and companies that make more money sharing, selling and releasing your personal information than they do having you as a customer. They want a part of that $2,000,000,000 and they obtain it at your expense by releasing your personal identifying information. We need to take a stand against this practice. The companies and businesses we are referring to are the ones that are not governed by any state or federal law that regulates or prohibits how they use our information once we provide it to them.

Some of the companies you deal with do not need any of your personal information. There are some businesses that may need some of your personal information; however, you can give them your private PO Box instead of your home address. As we stated earlier, you may not be able to stop them from sharing, selling or releasing your information, but you can control what personal information they have.

We need to talk about some examples of what happens to your personal information once you provide it to certain types of companies and businesses that you might have dealings with.

1. Discount cards from grocery stores or retail store cards - when you fill out an application for one of these cards, the business will store, share, sell and release the personal information you provide them on that application. These types of applications are not considered legitimate applications so we are not required to give them our information. Often times, you do not even need to fill out the application before being able to use the card, but if you are required to fill out the application prior, there is nothing that dictates you are required to give your true and accurate information.
2. Video rental stores – these stores ask for personal information as well. The reason given for needing this information is in case a customer skips out on returning rental movies. In this case, the company will have a way of initiating some type of recourse against that customer for the monetary loss. Video rental stores will also share, sell, and release your personal information you provide them so just make sure your address of record with them is your private PO Box and designated phone number.
3. Oil change stores – these stores will ask for your personal information and will share, sell and release it. If you feel it is necessary to give them any information other than your name, make sure it is your private PO Box and designated phone number.
4. Pizza delivery companies – these businesses sell their customer database. The information included in this database is the customers' name, home address, and home telephone number. We recommend you do not have pizza delivered to your home address but go pick it up instead. If you are going to try to protect your personal information, please be aware that the

pizza delivery companies will sell the information you provide them and it will show up in a number of databases that are accessible on the Internet. If you give them a fake name but still use your home address and phone number, queries into the Internet databases can still be made that will link the phone number to the address. The best way to prevent this is to order your pizza and go pick it up rather than giving the business any address at all.

5. Magazines – subscriber information is used to create mailing lists that are shared, sold, and released. We recommend you contact all the companies you receive magazines from, to include any mail order catalogs, and change your address to you private PO Box and give them your designated phone number. Most magazines and mail order companies do not give you the choice to opt-out of them sharing, selling or releasing your personal information. When you contact your magazine companies to change your address, ask what their privacy policy is and if you have any opt-out options. We have found that some do offer their customers this choice so just make sure you verify this with them so you are aware of their sharing practices.
6. Retail stores that ask for your phone number as you pay for your merchandise – it never ceases to amaze us the number of people who freely give out this information when the clerk asks them for it as they are paying at the register. These retail businesses will share, sell and release the information you give them as well as use it for marketing purposes. We do not recommend you give any personal information to a business when you are paying at the register. Please stop doing this. Retail businesses do not need any of our personal identifying information unless we have a line of credit through them at which time we can opt-out from them sharing and releasing it.

7. Business card in a jar for a free lunch – we most frequently see these jars in restaurants. We recommend you do not put one of your business cards in this jar. The restaurants generally make more money selling the information contained in that jar than they do supplying the winners with a free lunch.
8. Package shipping companies – If you are going to start protecting you home address, this is another method of dissemination you need to be aware of. The companies that ship our packages for us take the name and addresses of the sender and receiver and share, sell and release this information. This is one of the reasons why you can not have packages delivered to your residence. This information sharing could possibly open up your home address all over again in the areas you have worked so hard to have it removed. It does not matter who is sending you a package. Any and all packages need to be delivered to your private PO Box. When you are shipping a package, make sure you use your private PO Box as your return address. In the event this information does get released, by using your PO Box, it is at least not your home address.
9. Doctors' offices – there is absolutely no reason why your doctors' offices need your home address. We recommend you supply your private PO Box and your cell phone number as your contact information to all your doctors' offices, as well as the other family members' doctors, specialists, dentists, orthodontists, chiropractors, etc. Sometimes your doctors will file liens against you to ensure payment for services rendered. These medical liens are filed at the recorder's office which then makes them public record to include any of your personal identifying information that may have been included in the lien. If a medical lien is filed against you, the doctor uses what ever address they have on record for you. For this reason, change your address with all your doctors to your private PO

Box so your home address does not show up at the recorder's office as public record should this happen.

10. Warranty cards – you purchase a new appliance or other similar item and are given a warranty card in the information packet. If you do not fill out this card and mail it in, it will have absolutely no effect on your warranty. These cards are used for two purposes: 1) statistics and 2) information sharing.

We are certain you have many other companies and businesses you deal with on a regular basis that are similar to those we have just talked about. The reason we provided you the list in Chapter 3 was to make it easier for you to identify all these types of companies and businesses. It may take you some time, but once you have identified them, make sure you contact each one and get your personal information switched over to your private PO Box and your designated or contact phone number.

CHAPTER 9: LAW ENFORCEMENT PREVENTION TECHNIQUES

This chapter is written specifically for those individuals that work in the public service professions which include police officers, firefighters, court personnel, elected officials, etc. The information contained in this book pertains to anyone that is interested in protecting their personal identifying information from being released into public record and publicly available sources. The ideas we have discussed, however, may be more pressing and relevant for those that are out in the public's eye on a daily basis.

Death threats against police officers are quickly on the rise. Actual reported threats are up about fifty percent. One of the reasons why we believe these threats are on the rise is because it is easier for someone nowadays to locate a police officer away from the security of their job by just having their name.

Every officer receives threats from disgruntled citizens during the course of their regular duties. Most of these threats are made during the heat of the moment and are non-threatening to the officer. The citizen, as a general rule, has no intention of carrying out the threat. The officer realizes the subject is just venting so the officer does not feel it necessary to report the threat. These types of threats are considered a hazard of the job.

The types of threats that are on the rise are the ones officers give credibility to and believe are valid which causes the officers enough concern that they report it to their superiors. It is important for every police officer to know that their personal identifying information is released into public record and publicly available sources and how their information gets released. Because this phenomenon occurs, every police officer should start the protection process outlined in this book to further protect themselves and their families.

Threats against public officials and judges are also on the rise. Most individuals in these positions are elected which makes a majority of their information public record. It may be somewhat challenging to keep these individuals' information from getting into public record. For this type of protection to take place for these individuals, laws will need to change at all levels for this to be accomplished successfully.

Keeping Your Information Out of Public Record

Keeping personal identifying information out of public record and publicly available sources is extremely important for public service workers and will be a new way of life for those who choose these career paths. Police officers that started in this profession twenty years ago, before the invention of the Internet, did not have to worry about suspects locating them away from their job through easily accessible means. The increasing popularity of the Internet has changed all of this for our public service personnel. Easy accessibility to personal identifying information and learning how to protect this information will become their way of life and needs to be taught to all public service workers during the early stages of their career.

With the continuing growth of the Internet, every individual that works in public service needs to be concerned about their personal identifying information being available in public record and publicly available sources. They also need to be concerned with and understand how their personal information gets in publicly available information sources to include a variety of Internet databases. Along with understanding the how and why this happens, it is also essential they know what steps they can take to slow it down, if not completely stop it. The public service worker is constantly in the public eye and may never know when they upset someone to the point that the person will want to seek them out to cause harm to them or their family.

We recommend every police officer take our advice and go through what we describe as the protection process. Law enforcement officers tend to receive the most valid death threats. Other officials, such as political figures and judges, should take this matter seriously as well and initiate the protection process.

We also recommend fire fighters start taking the necessary steps to protect their personal information. Fire fighters do not routinely receive death threats during the course of their regular duties; however, they are constantly in public view. Because we can not predict the future, we recommend fire fighters do this as a preventative measure so if some type of threat were to be made, the fire fighter would already have this avenue of access protected.

If our public service personnel were to complete the protection process now when no emergency situation exists, they would be that much ahead of the game if and when the threat did come down. Taking these precautions now will ensure that when the Internet gets worse in the future, our public service professionals' personal information will not be available in public record and other publicly available information sources.

Record Redaction Laws

Back in 1997, the Arizona Legislature enacted state laws that allowed many who work in the public service professions within the State of Arizona to have their personal information redacted from certain public records. As these laws have evolved, what is now on the books provides a means for police officers, justices, judges, commissioners, public defenders, and prosecutors to have their records that are maintained by several state agencies sealed from public inspection.

The specific records the Arizona state law allows to be sealed from public inspection are an officer's Voter Registration records, Motor Vehicle Department records to include driver license as well as vehicle registration information, and records housed by the County Recorders, Assessors and Treasurers. This specific program is called the Peace

Officer Confidentiality Program and is available to current as well as retired officers. The Program is voluntary and an officer can have their records sealed until they request to be removed from the Program.

In researching other states to see if they have similar laws, we are discouraged to find that many do not. Redacting records is addressed as a state by state issue. If you are an officer in Arizona and have your records redacted but retire and move to another state that does not have these laws, the Arizona redaction will not cover you in the new state. If the state you moved to has these laws, you can submit the paperwork outlined in the process for that particular state to have your records sealed.

If you are a law enforcement officer in a state that does not have laws allowing you to redact your records, we strongly suggest you get with your department's attorney or legislative liaison/s and have them propose these potential laws to your State Legislature. This is an officer safety issue and needs to be addressed within each individual state.

To learn more about the Arizona Redaction Laws, we will have these specific laws linked through our website. You may access them and present them to your attorneys and/or liaisons to be used as an example.

We want to briefly mention Federal Agents because they are in a unique situation. Within Arizona, a peace officer is defined in the Redaction Laws as anyone who is vested by law to make arrests or has been vested by law. While assigned to a position in Arizona, Federal Agents qualify to have their records redacted. Because they can be re-assigned any where around the world at any given time, they will not always qualify for this protection once their residence is outside the State of Arizona. Our military police officers also find themselves in this same position. Because they generally are never stationed at any one place for a great length of time, they will not always have the protection these Arizona laws allow.

We have talked to and been in contact with many federal agents who have a concern for other agents that have received death threats.

If an agent re-locates from where they have received a threat and moves to a state without record redaction laws, they can not be protected in that state. To help secure the safety of all local, state, and federal law enforcement officers nationwide, it would be nice for laws similar to the Arizona Redaction Laws to be passed at a national level so each state would not have to address this issue on an individual basis. Having a law like this established at the Federal level would bring peace of mind to every law enforcement officer that no matter where they worked or lived they would have this little extra barrier of protection.

PART III: THE INTERNET'S ROLE IN PUBLIC RECORD

Introduction

In this section, we are going to discuss some basic concepts about the Internet that we feel are important as they relate to the protection process. The Internet in and of itself could be a topic for an entire book. We do not profess to be experts on how the Internet works or how it is set up. During our research, however, we have learned a few things about the Internet that we feel you need to know so you will have a better understanding of the role the Internet plays in the accessibility of your personal identifying information.

CHAPTER 10: PUBLIC RECORDS BEFORE AND AFTER THE INTERNET

Before the Internet

Our personal information has always been considered public record and publicly available. In a previous chapter, we talked about what it would take for someone to access our records prior to the Internet's popularity. Acquiring information generally took more time and energy on the requestor's part as they would have to go in person to submit their request. Because the process for obtaining the information was so involved, many people were unaware that they could actually obtain public record information or had any desire to do so. For this reason, many of us did not have the concern for protecting our personal information in the fore front of our minds.

After the Internet

With the invention of the Internet, government entities, businesses and companies were provided with an avenue to make public records and publicly available information sources that include our personal identifying information more readily accessible to the general public.

This practice of making public records available on the Internet is becoming more prevalent for those government entities that are tasked with maintaining documents that are open to public inspection. We also see all too often, on the television or in the newspaper, articles that talk about a new search engine or database that has surfaced on the Internet. The more we hear and read, the more we think the use of the Internet for this reason is out of control.

The Internet and what information it makes available is really bad right now. What will it be like in two, three or even five years? If the way it is right now is any indication of how it is going to be in the future, we are all going to be fighting an uphill battle with trying to keep our personal information protected.

As we have been teaching others on how to protect their personal information, we receive feedback from them all the time. One comment we frequently hear is from someone who has taken our advice and had their personal information removed from the websites included in our list, but run across a new website and find their personal information all over again.

We can not possibly give you every website that is in existence where your personal information may be found. What we are suggesting is that this is something you are going to have to stay on top of and continually pay attention to. Because technology changes so rapidly, there are always going to be new uses for the Internet. If after you complete the initial steps of the protection process, you find your personal identifying information somewhere else, you will need to do whatever it takes to have your information removed from there as well.

There are hundreds of databases on the Internet that store and keep our information. The smaller databases actually purchase information from the larger databases. This sharing can be a vicious cycle if you do not constantly monitor the sources where your information may be found. Because the Internet has given government and business such an easy avenue of access to the general public, we need to put the safety and security of our personal information in the fore front of our minds and keep it there. As we have previously stated, this is going to be a lifestyle change for many of us.

We all have different credit backgrounds, therefore, where we find our information is not necessarily where you will find yours. So, as you are surfing the web and you come across a website that has some of your personal identifying information, you need to research that specific website's privacy policy to find out how they got your information, what they do with it once they have it, if they offer you any opt-out options to have it removed and what can be done to stop them from sharing it.

Internet Databases

We are going to provide you with a list of databases we have identified during our research as the largest and most popular on the Internet. These databases are a great place to start with removing your personal identifying information from the Internet. You will need to send these databases an opt-out letter requesting they remove your personal information. We recommend you access each database, run your name and print what comes up. Highlight your information on the print out to include any current and old information that appears.

In your opt-out letter, specifically state you want everything you have highlighted on the print out removed from their database. You are going to send this print out as an attachment to your opt-out letter. Make sure in your letter you do not give them any information about you they do not already have. If they only have your name and addresses then just give them that information. Do not give them anything else like your date of birth or social security number.

Keep in mind, if you remove your information from these Internet databases and do not send your opt-out letters to the credit bureaus or stop using your home address on credit applications as we discussed in previous chapters, it will only be a matter of time before your information ends up right back on the Internet. It is essential you send opt-out letters to the credit bureaus prior to sending your letters to the Internet databases as most of the databases we are going to talk about purchase your information directly from the credit bureaus.

This is an important part of the process you need to understand and keep on top of. The chapters in this book and the check list outline the order we recommend you follow when completing the protection process. We also strongly suggest you periodically check these Internet databases to see if any of your personal identifying information has re-surfaced. Ultimately, it is up to you to stop this vicious information sharing cycle by utilizing all the steps we talk about in this book. If it has not occurred to you before now, let us say it again, once you complete the initial steps of the protection process, you are going to have to continually monitor this situation and do whatever it takes to maintain the integrity of your protected information.

At the time this book went to publication, we provided the most current privacy policies and opt-out requirements for each database we are going to individually discuss. Depending on when you read this book in relation to when it was published, these databases may have changed their opt-out requirements. Because over the past year we have seen many changes in the opt-out options on several of these databases, we recommend, prior to sending your opt-out letters, you go into each database and research their privacy policies to make sure you are following their current opt-out procedures. You need to do this research to ensure you are providing the database with what they need to accurately remove your personal information.

As we discuss each database, we are going to provide the database mailing address, the website address and directions on how to locate their privacy policies which should include their opt-out procedures. We are giving you instructions on how to find their privacy policies so you can see the similarities and the differences between these databases as well as familiarize yourself with searching these types of databases to gain a better understanding of how to find privacy policies on any new databases you may identify. We have also included a sample letter at the end of this chapter that you may use as a template for your opt-out letter or feel free to create your own.

ZABASEARCH

ZabaTools
2828 Cochran Street, #397
Simi Valley, CA 93065-2780

www.zabasearch.com – the first thing we want to show you on this website is where the privacy statement is so you can understand what their policy is for removing your information. The second thing we will explain is what you need to do to get your information removed.

Once on the website, run your first name, last name and put in the state where you live. All the records Zabasearch has on you will be displayed. When your information appears, scroll down to the bottom of that page. In small letters at the bottom, you will see an item that reads "Terms". If you click on this word, you will be taken to a pop up window. Scroll down towards the bottom until you see "ZabaTools Manage your Personal Information". Click on these words. Another window will appear that tells you to "click here". After clicking on the box, you will be taken to another window that will ask you for your e-mail address. The reason they ask you for your e-mail address is because they will e-mail you their privacy terms and what you need to do to have your information removed from their database. We are going to tell you how to have your information removed, but it is still a good idea for you to request their privacy terms anyway because Zabasearch has been known to frequently change their opt-out procedures so we recommend you double check.

ZabaTools is the company that will create, edit or delete your personal information maintained by Zabasearch. Zabasearch is a database that houses billions of free public records. This database can be queried for free and will provide an individual's addresses, phone numbers and month and year of birth. We recommend you have all your personal information, old and new, deleted from this database. Run yourself on the website to see what shows up under your first name, last name and the state you live in. We do not recommend you include any middle names when you make your inquiry. If you are a woman and have used different last names, query those names as well. If you have lived in other states, also run your name in those states.

You need to print out everything that comes up about you. Go through the list that comes up and highlight all the information relating to you. You need to mail these print outs as attachments to your opt-out letter. By sending the print outs, you will ensure all your addresses, current and past, are removed from the website. Make sure you specifically ask in your opt-out letter that all highlighted information be removed.

Zabasearch obtains their information from numerous sources; however, their main source is the credit bureaus. This is the reason why you need to make sure you get your permanent opt-out letters sent to the credit bureaus first. Anyone can request their personal information be removed from Zabasearch so run your family members and children. If you find any of their personal information, they should send in an opt-out letter as well.

PEOPLE FINDERS

Opt-Out PeopleFinders.com
1821 Q Street
Sacramento, CA 95814

www.peoplefinders.com – once on the home page of this website, scroll down to the bottom of the page where you will find a link that reads "Terms & Conditions". Clicking on these words will take you to another screen where you can read about the website's terms. As you scroll through the terms, towards the bottom, you will find an area that talks about what you need to do to have your information removed from this database.

This database is huge. It contains many records and links to previous addresses as well as other family members. Query the website by running your first name, last name and the state where you live. Once again, do not include any middle initials or names and run all previous names and states. Print out what information you do find and highlight the items that relate to you. You will want to mail this print out as an attachment with your opt-out letter.

What makes this website amazing is the amount of personal information you will find on your self as well as how it links you to your family members. These links are made to your family members from the information found on credit applications in the block that reads "list a relative not living with you" and from the credit bureaus.

MY FAMILY

MyFamily.com Inc.
Attention: Customer Solutions
360 West 4800 North
Prove, UT 84604

www.myfamily.com - This particular website is set up differently than any of the others we are going to talk about. My Family has several companies they are associated with it. The privacy policy specific to My Family is found if you click on "Privacy Policy" located at the bottom of the home page. On the next screen that appears, you will need to click on "MyFamily.com Privacy Policy" and read about what they do with the information they are provided and how to remove personal information from their database.

When you go into www.myfamily.com, at the top of the page, there are four tabs; My Site, MyFamily.com, Ancestry.com and People Finders. Through the My Site and MyFamily.com tabs is where you are able to create your own family website and connect with your family members. If you have any personal information in either of these locations, it is because you or one of your family members has put it there. This particular area on this website does not gather information from outside sources. Through the People Finder tab, you will be linked to the peoplefinder.com website we discussed earlier. Because it is the same website, you do not have to send another opt-out letter as you will have already done so.

The tab that you need to pay particular attention to is Ancestry.com. Click on this tab and query your name. We recommend that what ever personal information about you comes up, print it, highlight and send as an attachment with your opt-out letter.

PRIVATE EYE

Opt-Out PrivateEye.com
1223 Wilshire Boulevard, Suite 756
Santa Monica, CA 90403

www.PrivateEye.com – once on the home page for this website, you will find the word "Help" in the upper right hand corner. By clicking "Help", you will be linked to a page of frequently asked questions. Scroll through the questions until you see the Privacy and Security Section. In this section, you will get instructions on how to remove your personal information from this database.

As with the other databases we have already talked about, you need to query your name on this website. You will find this database looks very similar to People Finders, but it is different. Print any information that comes up reference your query, highlight all the information pertinent to you and include it as an attachment with your opt-out letter.

U.S. SEARCH

U.S. Search
Opt-Out Program
600 Corporate Point, Suite 220
Culver City, CA 90230

www.ussearch.com – once on this website, scroll down to the bottom of the home page and click on the link that reads "Privacy". You will be linked to a page that gives you information about this company and you will be provided instructions on how to remove your personal information from their database.

Query your name on this website to include any previous names used and any states you may have lived in. Follow the same steps for removing your personal information from this website as we have given you for all the other databases previously discussed. Make sure you print out, highlight all your information and mail in as an attachment with your opt-out letter.

INTELIUS

Intelius
500 108th Avenue NE, #1660
Bellevue, WA 98004

www.intelius.com – once on this website's home page, scroll down to the bottom and click on the word "Help". This will take you to another page where you will need to scroll through the section on "Privacy Frequently Asked Questions" until you find "How can I remove my information from the Intelius public record database?" The answer to this question will explain what you need to do to have your personal identifying information removed from their database.

Intelius is very similar to all the other websites in that you can query your name to see what information about you is housed in their database. Print out what ever pertinent information you find that applies to you so you can include this as an attachment with your opt-out letter.

Intelius requires you complete an additional step in their opt-out procedure. They want you to either provide them a copy of your driver license, after blacking out your driver license number and photo or if you do not want to give them a copy of your driver license, you will need to have your opt-out letter notarized. To remove your information, they will accept either the copy of the driver license or the notarized letter. Intelius wants you to fax your opt-out request with any attachments to a number provided on their website instead of sending it through the mail.

The last database we are going to talk about, Lexis Nexis, limits who they will allow to have information removed from their public and non-public information databases. The only groups of individuals who can opt-out at this website are law enforcement officers or public officials, identity theft victims and any others who are at risk of physical harm. People in general can not have their personal identifying information removed from this database. Lexis Nexis is a good example of a non-public information source that is privately owned which enables them to place more stringent restrictions on who can have their personal information removed.

LEXIS NEXIS

Lexis Nexis Opt-Out
PO Box 933
Dayton, OH 45401

www.lexisnexis.com – on the home page of this website, click on the block that reads "Go to U.S. Home". On the page that appears, scroll down to the bottom and click "Privacy & Security". This will take you to another page, where you will see on the right hand side an option that reads "Requesting Opt-Out". Clicking on this option will take you to a page that explains who can opt-out of this database and what specific procedures need to be followed.

For those groups of people who qualify to have their information removed from this database, there are forms that are specific to each group that need to be printed and filled out.

1. If you are a victim of identity theft there is a form called an identity theft affidavit that you will need to fill out and mail along with a copy of the police report showing you have been a victim of identity theft.
2. If you are in danger of physical harm, you will need to provide a copy of a police report or protective court order that has been issued along with the explanation of reason form and opt-out template.
3. If you are a law enforcement officer, you will find three forms (an explanation of the reason, a letter from a supervisor that actually needs to be signed by your supervisor and the opt-out template) that you will need to print, fill out, and mail in. These forms will allow you to have your personal information removed from the public record and non-public record databases maintained by Lexis Nexis.
4. If you are a public official or your position exposes you to a threat of death or serious bodily harm, you will need to fill out the explanation of reason form along with the opt-out template.

Lexis Nexis feeds their database information into several other large paid databases such as Autotrack and Accurint.

On-Line Opt-Out Options

We have previously discussed three on-line opt-out options; however, we would like to further talk about what these websites are going to look like once you access them on the Internet.

THE DIRECT MARKETING ASSOCIATION

www.the-dma.org – once on this website's home page, scroll down to the bottom and click on "Privacy Statement". From here, you click on "Privacy Policy for Consumers". This will take you to the page that provides all the information and opt-out options offered by the Direct Marketing Association. You will be given three options that will take your name, address, phone numbers and e-mail addresses off marketing lists which will help cut back on the amount of junk mail and telemarketing calls you receive. We recommend you click in to all three links that are provided to remove your name from mailing lists, to get your name off telemarketing lists and to get your name off e-mail lists.

To exercise these three options, you will need to supply various items of your personal identifying information. Once you do this, you will be given two options on how to submit your requests. If you want to submit the form you fill out directly on-line, you will have to pay a charge to use this method. If you want to submit your request by sending it through the mail, you will print the form you filled out on-line and send it to the address provided. This mail in option can be completed at no charge.

OPT-OUT PRESCREEN

www.optoutprescreen.com – on this website's homepage, scroll down to the bottom of the page to the block that reads "Click Here to Opt-In or Opt-Out". On the next page, we recommend you click the dot next to permanent opt-out choice and then click "Submit". You will be prompted on the next page to fill in the blanks with various items of your personal identifying information to include a security code. When you click confirm, you will be given a form you need to print, sign and mail to the address they provide.

This website was designed so people would have an easy and convenient method to permanently opt out of receiving pre-screened offers of credit and insurance. We recommend you complete this opt-out option along with mailing in your opt-out letters to the three credit bureaus we discussed in Chapter 7.

THE DO NOT CALL REGISTRY

www.donotcall.gov – This is the website where you can register your home and cell phone numbers to request not to receive telemarketing calls. Keep in mind that this is not a cure all for stopping telemarketing calls. Even after registering your phone numbers on this website, you may still receive calls that originate from out of the country, exempt organizations, or random dial calls. Once you are on this website, take the time to read the information it provides as it will explain what they are trying to accomplish by having you register your phone numbers.

By providing you with details about the largest and most popular databases found on the Internet that make your personal identifying information available, we have given you a good starting point with removing your information off of the Internet. As we stated early on in this chapter, we can not give you a listing of every Internet database that is in existence. What we can do is you give the advice that if you do come across another source on the Internet that contains your personal identifying information, take action by reading their privacy policy and doing whatever it takes to have your information removed.

Sample Opt-Out Letter

<DATE>

<ADDRESS>

To Whom It May Concern:

I request to have my personal information redacted from your public record database as soon as possible. Below is the information that I would like to be redacted. I have also printed up and highlighted all information I would like to have removed. I appreciate your cooperation in this matter. If you have any questions or concerns, I can be reached at *(XXX) XXX-XXXX.*

Sincerely,

<NAME>

Please remove the following information on:

<NAME>
<ADDRESS> (list all of your addresses you wish to have removed)

I have provided links in the following pages with information that I would like to have removed from this website.

CHAPTER 11: THE INTERNET TODAY

Public Records on the Internet Today

Hopefully with the information we have covered in the previous chapters, we have successfully captured your attention about the easy accessibility of your personal identifying information on the Internet and how it can be obtained by anybody who has the desire to seek it out. Now that your interest has been piqued about this subject matter, we sincerely hope you have started to implement the steps we recommend to better protect you and your family.

During your implementation of the protection process, you should have spent some time already on the Internet researching yourself and your family members. You probably are in awe and amazed with what personal information you were able to find. In writing this book, we have spent many hours on the Internet searching for people's personal information. We are astounded with what types of information is available and what we have found on ourselves as well as our family members. We have seen many changes take place with the Internet and have watched its tremendous growth over the past couple years. The Internet is a great tool but like so many other great things, its greatness can also negatively impact innocent others. As far as we are concerned, because we see how it can jeopardize a person's safety with respect to our personal identifying information being placed on the Internet, this practice is out of control. We need to be creative and pull out all the stops to slow this down.

In the next chapter, we are going to talk about the future of the Internet, but for now we need to discuss what is currently taking place. The whole Internet concept is great in so many ways, but the downside is what we need to be aware of.

Public Records in the Different States

In this section, we are going to provide you with some websites that will enable you to search your specific state to see what is considered public record and to find which of these records are accessible on the Internet. Each individual state has their own laws and views on what is considered "open" records and "closed" records. You need to know the laws in your state and understand what is considered public record and open to public inspection. In many instances, the items your state considers public record are what is being put on the Internet.

In Arizona, as an example, the documents housed with the various County Recorder's, Assessor's and Treasurer's Offices and the Corporation Commission (statewide) are considered public record and are made accessible on the Internet. Each of these government entities has their own website in which these documents can be easily queried and viewed.

State Search Websites

www.state.XX.us – Replace the XX with your state's abbreviation. This is the main website for your state and it should be the first website you check. Querying this website is a good place to start the research for the state where you live. It will give you some basic information about your state and what is considered public record.

www.searchsystems.net – This website is set up so you can query each individual state and it will explain what records within that state are considered public record. When you get onto the website home page, scroll down until you get to the section titled "United States by State". Within this section is where you will click on your state which will take you to another page. On this page, you will find numerous links to other websites specific to the entities within your state's government that house documents considered public record. This website is another great place to start researching your particular state to see what is considered public record.

www.50states.com - This website also provides information about the individual states. You will find links to other websites sponsored by the various government entities within your state where you will find basic information about your state to include its history.

www.brbpub.com/pubrecsites.asp - This is another website that allows you to research state by state. When you get onto the homepage, under the section "Free Government Public Record Sites", click on the link "State, County and City Sites". On the page that appears, click on your particular state which will bring up a list of all the records that are currently accessible on the Internet. If one of the named websites does not offer records directly on-line, it will provide instructions on how you can obtain records from them by submitting a request in person, through the mail or by fax. This website is a great tool for researching what records your state puts directly on the Internet and to determine the other avenues you can use to obtain those records not available via the Internet.

In addition to researching the state where you live for public records, we strongly encourage you to query your name through any and all search engines you find on the Internet. There are things you can do in your personal life that will end up in public record, publicly available information sources and on the Internet. Some examples of this could be a write up about you by an educational institution, an article in a publication (newspaper, magazine) in which you are named, or accomplishments achieved in a particular sport to name just a few.

www.google.com – Google is a very popular and well known website. It is a great place to start your search on the Internet with trying to find other places where you or your personal information may be found.

We are going to tell you about a basic search technique that will help you refine your searches and find those records specific to your subject matter. This search technique is commonly referred to as a Boolean search. We are not going to cover this technique in depth but there are some basics on Boolean searching that we feel will be beneficial to you.

Boolean Searches

Boolean searching is based on a system of symbolic logic more universally known as just plain algebra. Most computer databases, Internet websites and search engines support this keyword logic search concept. When querying a search engine on the Internet, your results will depend on how you combine keywords together. The main purpose for using a Boolean type search technique is to perform accurate searches without producing irrelevant results.

The below information was taken from the Lake Sumter Community College website, http://www.lscc.edu/library/guides/boolsea.htm. This website contains a wealth of information and provides excellent explanations on the different types of Boolean searches.

Samples of Boolean Searches:

AND

Using AND between keywords will help narrow your search by combining the terms. Running your search using this method will retrieve every document that contains both of the words specified.

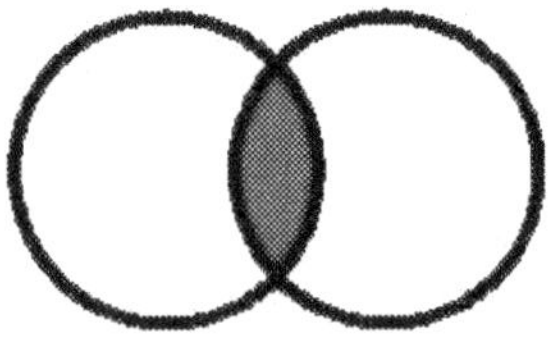

Internet **AND** ***security***

To help understand the Boolean concept, you need to be aware of what will show up in your search results if you do not use AND between your keywords. If you were to just run the words Internet security, your results would include every Internet article that contains the word Internet and every article that contains the word security. The size of your results list would be enormous.

Get on-line and try these types of searches. Run the words as such: Internet security. Next, run the words with the AND in between them. Run Internet and security. Do you see the difference between the number and quality of the results? Try other combinations of words.

OR

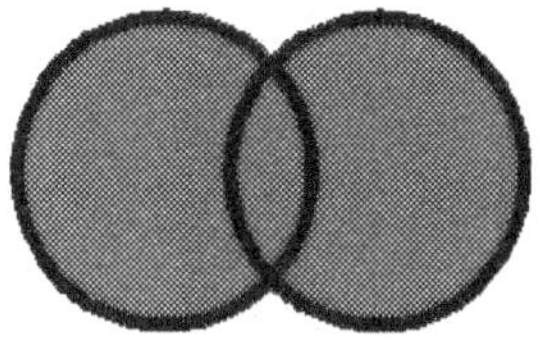

Weightlifting* OR *Bodybuilding

Using OR between your keywords will broaden or widen your search. Your results will include documents containing either keyword. This search method is useful when there are several synonyms for a concept or a variant spelling of a word.

NOT

Using NOT between your keywords will narrow your search by excluding unwanted terms.

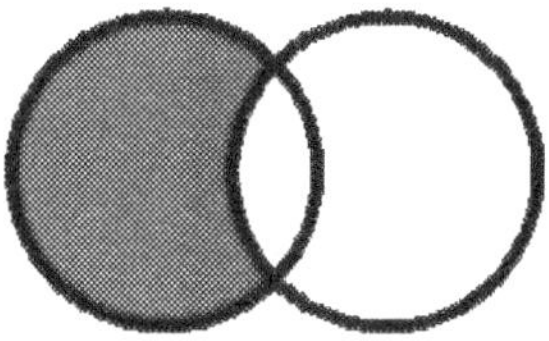

Gambling* NOT *Lottery

NEST

When conducting complex searches, you can use more than one operator and can NEST your search terms. Nesting is an advanced search technique and is mostly used when there are numerous ways to address a topic. The search terms and operators included in parentheses will be searched for first.

(ADD OR Attention Deficit Disorder) AND College Students

QUOTES

Using QUOTES will allow you to search for a specific phrase, not just individual words. If you run web design, your results will include every web page that contains the word web and every web page that contains the word design. You will get thousands of hits by running these two words in this manner.

Now, if you run "web design", your results will be all the web pages where the words web design appear together. This method helps narrow your search to the exact words you are looking for.

+ SYMBOL

By using a plus sign and adding additional descriptors to your keywords, you can narrow your search even more. This is the search method we recommend you use when running your name. After your name, add the plus symbol and any words that might be associated with you like AZ, police, biking, teacher, diving, etc. When selecting what descriptors to run behind your name, use your work, your hobbies, or anything you are involved in that may have records about you that might show up on the Internet. Make sure you run your family members, including your children, to see what items are found on the Internet about them.

"John Smith" + police
"Jane Doe" + scuba
"Frank Doe" + 5K

* Asterisk Wild Card

The asterisk can be used as a substitute for any amount of letters in a word. Using this method to search is useful because the results will include all words with a specific root and any suffix that can be attached to it.

Stat* Status - Statistics - Statistician

By using Stat*, your results will be similar to the words displayed above. In our example, we only display 3 results. If you actually ran Stat* on the Internet, many more hits would be received. With using this wild card search technique, you need to be careful and know exactly what you are looking for so you can narrow the results you are going to get.

Surfing the Web: Search Engines

There are too many search engines for us to name that can be found on the Internet. We recommend when you run across one or are told about one, you query your self and your family members to see if any information about you or them can be found. Start with www.google.com since it is one of the biggest and most popular. Some of the items you can run include:

- Name
- Phrases (words of songs…)
- Telephone numbers XXX-XXX-XXXX or all together XXXXXXXXXX
- E-mail addresses
- Home Address

The main purpose behind doing these queries is to learn what is available on the Internet about you and your family. If you do not find anything, that is great. If you do locate an item and can identify the source behind why it is on the Internet, make contact with that source to see if there is anything you can do to have it removed so it will no longer be available for viewing.

CHAPTER 12: THE FUTURE...

Where are Public Records Heading?

This may be a short chapter, however, it contains some important information we need to shed some light on. We have absolutely no idea what the Internet is going to be like in the future. We can only speculate and we do believe it is going to get worse.

Over the past five years, we have seen many, many changes with the Internet that we can only surmise the changes will continue to take place at an alarming rate. Within other schools of thought, we have the ability to take a look at what has happened in the past, which allows us to study the path that was traveled to get to the present. Based on this path, we should be able to estimate and project the direction the path will follow in the future. When we try to apply this way of thinking to the Internet, we can not fathom what the Internet will be like in two, three or even five years. To try to make sense of something that is out of control right now and attempt to comprehend what it will be like in the future is unimaginable to us.

The general consensus, we believe, is that the Internet is going to get worse. We are living during a time where there is a minimal expectation of privacy as it involves our personal identifying information maintained by companies and businesses we have financial relationships with. What we have tried to stress throughout this book is that if you can understand what is taking place with your personal identifying information and its availability on the Internet, you are in a better position to take control of this situation. If you can not stop the government, private businesses and companies from sharing your information, you can at least control what information they have available to release. Each and every one of us needs to take a stand and make a statement to these entities that are sharing, selling and releasing our personal identifying information. We can guarantee the release of our personal information is only going to get worse as time goes on.

Throughout this book, we have talked about the protection process and the numerous steps you can take to slow down, if not completely stop this information sharing cycle. We realize there will be some circumstances in which you will be unable to stop the release of your personal information completely; however, you do have the ability to control what information is available in the event it does get released.

If you start the protection process now, control what information you provide your creditors and exercise the available opt-out options, you may have a chance of controlling what is being released. If your information is being sold and released, at least it is your private PO Box and not your home address. You also need to follow through with our recommendation to remove what information is already out there on you and your family members. We discussed this step of the protection process in Chapter 10 which covered the database searches and opt-out letters.

Even after this book is published, we will discover new databases and new avenues that are being used to disseminate our personal identifying information. What we are suggesting is that you use this book as a guide and a learning tool to help understand how your personal identifying information was released in the first place, know you can remove what is currently available on the Internet, know you can get your creditors to stop sharing, selling and releasing your personal information and be well informed about this information sharing industry so you can start to take a stand with those companies and businesses you choose to start a relationship with in the future. Remember, starting and maintaining the protection process will be a life style change for many of us and a way of life for our children.

At this point in time, the steps that make up what we describe as the protection process are working. We know many individuals who have taken our advice and have implemented the steps discussed in this book. Thus far, it does work. They are very well protected as their information is not found on any database and their creditors are not sharing, selling or releasing their personal information.

CHAPTER 13: CHANGING THE LAWS

The topics we have talked about in this book can be extremely overwhelming if this is the first time you have heard about them. It is new information for many of us and is critical to our safety and security.

Right now, we are standing at a threshold trying to look into the future. Do the laws need to change so that our personal identifying information is better protected? ABSOLUTELY! Will these changes take place over night or within the next couple of years? PROBABLY NOT! Do we even have the power to affect this kind of change? WE DO NOT KNOW! Do we, as citizens of the United States, need to take a stand against the release of our personal identifying information and identity theft? YES! Do we need to stand up to try to make changes? YES! Do personnel within the public service professions need to be concerned their personal information is available in public record and on the Internet? ABSOLUTELY!

This current state of affairs affects each and every one of us and will continue to do so as we head into the future. Coping with public record and the Internet is our way of life from this point forward. We need to learn as much as we can about it and adjust to it.

What is Needed for Change?

We can all agree that change needs to take place and laws need to be passed to control the release of our personal information. Any new laws passed need to restrict companies and businesses from considering our personal information publicly available and prohibit its release for profit. Business entities need to be held accountable for releasing our personal identifying information. Engaging in this information sharing practice without our knowledge needs to be stopped dead in its tracks. We, as consumers, should be offered an "opt-in" option rather than an "opt-out" option. We, as consumers, need to speak out and let our voices be heard. We need to let companies and businesses know that our personal information is not a matter of public record or publicly available and they need to stop sharing, selling and releasing it.

Identity theft is beyond being out of control and the easy accessibility of our personal identifying information is one of the main reasons why. When someone can find all the necessary information on the Internet that is needed to steal or take over an identity, a major problem exits. Billions of dollars are lost every year due to identity theft and the losses will continue to skyrocket.

Writing to Your Elected Officials

One of the best ways to have our voice heard is by contacting our elected officials. Since most citizens do not realize information sharing is the problem that it actually is, it is almost guaranteed that our government officials do not understand the magnitude of this problem either. The only people, who seem to understand this issue is those who work in the information sharing industry, those who see it while conducting their normal work duties or those that have become victims of identity theft.

Based on history, we have learned that change can be affected if enough people stand up and voice their concerns to our elected officials. A website is available on the Internet that lists all the local, state, and federal level elected officials. We recommend you access this website and query your state to identify who your elected officials are.

The website where you can research your elected officials is www.congress.org. Once on the website's home page, you will find an area on the upper left side that reads "Write Your Officials". In this block, you will need to enter your zip code and click on the search button. When your list of federal elected officials appears, you will be shown two contact options below their name. One tab will read "e-mail" and the other "info". If you click on the "info" button, you will be given the address where you can send a letter to that particular official. We recommend you write them a letter. From the screen where your federal officials are listed, you are given two other tabs that will take you to information about your state and local elected officials. In this information, you should find instructions on how to make contact with them.

Please understand that we are encouraging you to write to your elected officials expressing your concerns about your personal identifying information being shared, sold and released by companies and businesses and how this information is ending up on the Internet. In your letters, if you wish, you can also express your concern about how this information sharing is contributing to the identity theft crisis.

We are hoping if our elected officials receive enough correspondence that expresses these concerns, they will take note of it and actively work towards changing the privacy laws. As we stated earlier, we are not going to see any changes occur overnight, but if our elected officials start hearing from their constituents that they have this strong concern then just maybe we will see some changes made to the privacy laws at some point in the future.

PART IV: IDENTITY THEFT

Introduction

We are not going to spend a great deal of time talking about identity theft. We do, however, feel like we need to touch on some basics as our protection process does go hand in hand with this crime. We did not design this book to be used solely as an aid once someone has become a victim. Our purpose for writing this book is for it to be used as a prevention tool from becoming an identity theft victim.

If you start the protection process and complete all the steps we have discussed, your information will be protected in ways that will prevent identity theft from happening in the first place. As the Internet gets worse and your information is being released into public record and publicly available information sources, the protection process steps are not going to be a cure all for identity theft. If you step up and take charge of your own identity and follow through with the necessary steps to prevent your personal identifying information from getting into publicly available information sources and on the Internet, you will be way ahead of the identity thieves.

CHAPTER 14: PREVENT BECOMING A VICTIM

Pay Attention to Your Information

Throughout this book, we have provided you with numerous strategies that will help you start protecting your personal information. The bottom line is you need to take charge and be in control of your own information. It would be ideal if the privacy laws were changed to assist us with protecting our personal information, but ultimately, it is each of our own responsibility.

Everything we have talked about so far is preventative. The strategies outlined in this book were not intended to help you recover once you have become a victim of identity theft. The steps of our protection process were designed to help protect your personal information and remove it from public record and publicly available information sources before you even become a victim. This book will help you with preventing your personal information from being stolen. If you are one of the unfortunate Americans that have had their identity stolen, these strategies are great to implement in addition to all the other steps you are going to have to take because you have been an identity theft victim. Use this book as a prevention tool, after you have recovered your identity, so you will not be as likely to become a repeat victim.

If you complete the steps we have talked about in this book, it will be much harder for the thieves to get your personal information and take over your identity. Our protection process is not going to stop identity theft but, if we can just make it that much harder for the thieves, why would we not want to take these precautions? We need to protect ourselves from the criminals who prey on people for new identities to steal.

Another suggestion we like to make while you are paying attention to your information is to start using a safe at your house to help store and secure your important items. We highly recommend you do this. Make sure the safe you use is fastened to the floor so it will be harder for someone to grab and move. Keep all your important documents in the safe to include social security cards, birth certificates, marriage or divorce records, credit cards, unused checks, or any other item you want secured. Do not leave these types of items lying around or in an unsecured filing cabinet.

Another concern you need to be aware of is never give your personal identifying information out over the telephone or in response to an e-mail unless you originated the contact with the requesting company or business. We have heard story after story about people who have received a phone call from an individual claiming they are with a "particular company". It just so happens the "particular company" is one that the victim does do business with on a regular basis. The victim is made to feel comfortable enough by the caller and ends up giving out the personal information being requested.

Please do not do this. If the caller sounds legitimate, ask for their name, an identifying number such as an employee number, and a call back number. Verify who they are by calling the company back before you give out any information whatsoever over the telephone or via e-mail. These types of calls and e-mails are almost always scams and the person receiving the call will usually end up becoming a victim of identity theft.

Pay Attention to Your Spending

Ideally, paying cash for everything is the best option. If you are like most Americans, this is not feasible so you find yourself using debit and credit cards.

First, let us talk about your checking account and your debit card usage. We recommend you keep your debit receipts until they clear your account. We also recommend you check your account daily or at least every two to three days. If a charge is trying to clear your account and you did not make that purchase, it is better to catch it early and get action started through your bank or credit union.

We hear conflicting stories all the time about how it is not a good idea to always use your debit card or conversely, how it is safer to use the debit card rather than write a check. We really do not have an opinion one way or the other on this issue. If you are in the habit of monitoring your checking account daily, go ahead and continue to use your debit card. If you feel more comfortable writing checks, continue to write checks. You need to go with what you feel safe doing.

Society, in general, is moving away from the practice of writing checks. If you find you have to write a check, use a gelled ink pen. These pens make it harder for the thieves to wash off the ink and re-write the check. It is still possible for the thieves to wash the check, but it involves extra steps and is much harder, as well as time consuming, to complete.

You need to make sure you are shredding all previous years returned or carbon copy checks in your possession. There is no reason why you need to keep them. Most banks and credit unions are not returning cancelled checks to their customers any more and are made available only by request. If you do have old returned or carbon copy checks, we recommend you have a shredding party.

We are not aware of any rule of thumb on how long cancelled checks need or should be kept. If the checks have cleared your account and the creditor is not disputing the transaction, we do not see a need to keep them. If you feel more comfortable keeping them, start with the last three years and shred the previous years. This will be a great place to start, after which you can monitor your need to keep them. Eventually though, you will need to shred them all.

Next, we need to talk about your credit cards. We definitely recommend you keep all your charge receipts until they post to and clear your account. After this time, if you will not need the receipt for a product return or proof of purchase, you can shred them. If any charges show up on your bill that you are not familiar with, call the creditor as most will have additional information about each transaction. Check and verify that each transaction appearing on your bill is one you authorized and are familiar with.

We also strongly recommend that you do not carry all of your credit cards on your person, in your purse or wallet, at any one time. Keep your credit cards stored in a safe at your home. If you need to use a credit card, retrieve the one for the transaction at hand and when done, put the card back in the safe.

Paying bills on-line is another concern we are frequently asked about. We pay our bills on-line all the time and have never experienced any problems. It is a nice convenience to have the option of paying your bills directly and not have to worry about writing a check, making sure you have a stamp, and getting it to the post office within enough time so the payment is not late. We like to have this control of our bills and be able to pay them at our leisure.

The only advice we can give you about paying your bills on-line is to go with your gut feeling. If the website is secure and it is one of your creditors you know, you should not experience any problems. Call your creditors to ensure their website is secure if you have any doubts.

CHAPTER 15: SHREDDING YOUR INFORMATION

Why Shred?

This is another short chapter but still a very important one. Our goal is to stress the importance of shredding any item that has your personal information on it before throwing it away and encouraging each and every household nationwide to have a personal shredder with family members actually using it.

If there is any one thing we can suggest to help you not become a victim of identity theft, it would be shredding your personal information before you throw it in the trash. Shredders are usually priced from $15 to $50 for the smaller ones designed for home use. The benefits of this purchase will far out weigh the cost. Buy a shredder for your house and use it. We recommend getting a cross-cut shredder so the papers are cut into smaller pieces which makes it harder for someone to piece back together.

Once you have a shredder, use it for everything. Go through all your mail every day. If a piece of mail has your name and/or address on it, shred it. From this point forward, you should not put anything of a personal identifying nature into the trash without it first being shredded.

Dumpster Divers

As we previously stated, we recommend you shred everything with your name and address on it. Do not even throw junk mail in the trash without shredding your name and address. There are people who go through dumpsters and trash cans to find names, addresses, social security numbers and dates of birth on papers that have been thrown away. The people who engage in this activity are called dumpster divers. These people do this for a living and are making lots of money removing our personal information from the trash and taking over our identities.

If everybody would start shredding their trash, we could put the dumpster divers out of business. Shredding items containing our personal information would eliminate another source of accessibility for our information. Shredding will also ensure the safety of our information in the event our trash is rummaged through by a dumpster diver.

CHAPTER 16: ONCE YOU HAVE BECOME A VICTIM

This book has been designed to shed some light on prevention methods that can help curb identity theft. We believe, however, that identity theft awareness should also be addressed in this book since our protection process and identity theft is inter-related. This crime alone is out of control and is projected to get worse in the future. Suspects, who make this their crime of choice, are making more money taking over our identities than they would make if they were to commit a robbery. Also, the chances of an identity theft suspect getting caught is slim to none. These cases have a tendency to be very difficult and complex and often times, can take many years to bring to a conclusion.

We have stressed that you need to take control of your own personal information so it does not get sold and released into public record, publicly available information sources and on the Internet. You also need to take control of your information and do whatever it takes to prevent your identity from being stolen. As with the protection process, there are steps that you can and must take to safeguard your own personal identifying information from being taken over by another individual.

If you have been a victim of identity theft, you know there are many things you need to take care of to recover your identity. The procedures for this process alone are another book all by itself. We are not going to focus on the identity recovery process, but we would like to point you in the direction of where to go to acquire information about this particular process. This is another area where you need to take the time to research and understand the procedures that need to be completed if you ever do become a victim. If you take the time to research this matter, you will be better prepared to understand the topics we discuss in this book and you will have a head start with knowing what your creditors and the credit bureaus will need should you ever become an identity theft victim.

As you are making contact with your creditors during the different stages of the protection process as we have previously discussed, we have another question we want you to ask them. You need to ask your creditors what information they have available and what procedures they have implemented on the prevention and recovery of identity theft. Ask if they have any documents or pamphlets that explain their procedures in writing they can send to you. Generally speaking, your credit card companies will usually have their own prevention and recovery steps you need to follow if you ever become a victim.

You should find the credit bureaus also have information published on identity theft. During your contacts with the credit bureaus, ask what they have available for you to read. The more information you can get your hands on about the prevention and recovery of identity theft the better off you will be to prevent it and the better prepared you will be in the event you do find yourself a victim.

Steps to Take

There are several steps you need to take once you realize you have had your identity stolen. It is important to make sure you complete each and every one.

1. The first and most important step you need to do once you have discovered you have been a victim of identity theft is to call and get a police report. Without a police report, most creditors will not do anything to assist you.
2. The next step is to contact the fraud departments of each credit bureau. Ask that fraud alerts be placed on your credit reports. The credit bureaus absolutely need to know you have been a victim of identity theft. At this time, we also recommend you obtain current copies of your credit reports, one from each

bureau, to see if any new accounts have been opened without your knowledge or authorization.

- Trans Union -- 1-800-680-7289
- Equifax -- 1-800-525-6285
- Experian -- 1-888-397-3742

3. Contact your bank, credit union and every creditor. You may need to close or cancel any credit cards you may have. Your creditors will walk you through the steps to have your account restricted or closed and get it set up so you can start using it again.
4. Contact the Federal Trade Commission (FTC). They keep a secure victim database that law enforcement has access to. If your case is similar to others, this may be a great way to make sure the cases get connected. It may also assist law enforcement officers, who locate suspects, with identifying you and tracking you down as one of their victims.
    a. www.ftc.gov
    b. FTC's Identity Theft Hotline -- 1-877-438-4338
    c. www.consumer.gov/idtheft
5. Keep copies of everything. Write down dates, times and people's names you have contacted through out the process of notifying your creditors and the credit bureaus. Keep a log of all your contacts and copies of what you receive. This will help keep you organized, plus it may help in your case should the police ever catch the suspect. Keep, save and write down absolutely everything.

Common Sense Food for Thought

There are other tid bits of information we think are common sense but, we feel we need to reiterate them here as a reminder.

- ✓ Protect your PIN numbers and keep them in a secure place, such as in your safe. Create unique passwords; do not use common passwords such as your date of birth or your house numbers. Always remember; never give out your pin numbers for your accounts to anyone under any circumstances.
- ✓ Take out going mail directly to the post office instead of leaving it in the mailbox at your house. Thieves will search for mailboxes that have the red flag raised. Do not leave incoming mail in the mail box at your home over night. We highly recommend you check your house mailbox daily. If you are going to be out of town, put a hold on your mail with the Post Office. Utilizing a private PO Box will minimize the need for you to take these actions.
- ✓ Never give out your personal information over the phone unless you initiated the call. Be wary of unsolicited calls in which they ask you for your personal information.
- ✓ Store all your personal documents in a safe in your house; making sure the safe is fastened to the floor.
- ✓ Review your bank and credit card statements every month.
- ✓ Use your shredder.
- ✓ If your social security number is used as your driver license number, go to your motor vehicle department and get a department-issued generic number. Do not have your social security number associated with your driver license at all.
- ✓ Carry your purse or wallet on your person at all times. Ladies, do not leave your purse in the shopping cart at the grocery store. Do not leave your purse or wallet in your car when you go into the day care center to drop off or pick up your children. Do not leave your purse or wallet in your vehicle when you go into the gym to workout. Thieves know this happens and will target these locations.

- ✓ On your checks, only have your first and middle name initials listed with your last name. Do not have your full name, phone number or social security number printed on your checks.
- ✓ Also, when writing out a check, do not put the full account number on the memo line. Use a partial account number or do not list one at all.
- ✓ On the back of your credit cards put that you wish them to ask for identification. You can use the words; Check ID or Photo ID Required.
- ✓ Photo copy everything in your wallet or purse and keep the copies in a safe place. If your wallet or purse is stolen, you will have the necessary contact information readily accessible and an itemized list of exactly what was in your wallet or purse. You can even keep one set of copies at work and one set at home.

Closing Remarks

In closing, we would like to thank you for taking the time to listen to our message. We wish you the best of luck during your endeavor with protecting you and your family members' personal information. Please visit our website at www.personalinfoprotection.com to see what current helpful hints and tips we will continually make available reference the protection process. All of the forms mentioned throughout the chapters will also be available on our website so, if you prefer, you can work with an electronic copy. Since maintaining the integrity of your protected information is now going to be your way of life, we encourage you to keep our website in your list of favorites on your computer.

As we have stated before, we are constantly learning new things about this personal information protection process. If during your experiences you come across a new piece of information, a new database, have a success story or a horror story; please do not hesitate to let us know by contacting us through our website. We are definitely interested in any feedback from those who are taking our advice and embarking on this new way of life.

PART V: CHECK LIST

We have put together a check list of the steps that you must take to start the protection process. Keep in mind that this is a process and each step must be completed if you truly want to protect your personal identifying information.

_ Check list

_ _ Get your Private PO Box set up, Chapter 4.
- This address looks like an apartment complex address.

_ _ Make a list of all your creditors, Chapter 3.
- Those businesses you pay money to every month or year.
- Those businesses you receive statements from every month or year.
- Those accounts that are open on your credit report.

_ _ Call each and every one of your creditors, Chapter 6.
- Use the list of creditors you have been working on through out the book.
- Have them tag your account to not share, sell or release your personal identifying information.
  - They may do this over the phone.
  - They may require you to mail them a letter.
  - They may mail you an opt-out form that you will need to fill out and mail back.
- Change your address with your creditors to your Private PO Box.
  - Those that do not need your home address; give them your private PO Box and use it like your home address.

    - Those that need your home address for service, make sure they have your private PO Box as your mailing address and ensure all mail goes to the PO Box and not to your home address.

_ _ List of businesses you do businesses with on a daily, monthly and yearly basis, Chapter 3.

- As you do your business with them, start changing your address to your private PO Box and provide your designated phone number.

_ Pull your credit reports.

- Learn how to read your credit report.
    - The credit bureaus have guides on how to understand your credit report.
- Control what accounts you have open and closed.
    - If you wish to close any old accounts, do so but make sure you do it at a time when you will not need your credit.
    - Contact those creditors you want to close accounts through.
    - Write a letter to the credit bureaus stating you want to close these account to have them shown as closed on your credit report.
- Write your letter to the credit bureaus so they will not share, sell or release your personal identifying information.

_ Write and send the opt-out letters to the Internet databases, Chapter 10.

- Get on-line and research yourself through each listed database
- Complete your opt-out letters

- Mail letters and additional print outs from the databases

_ Complete on-line opt-out forms and send, Chapter 10.
- Complete and mail forms for www.the-dma.org.
- Complete and mail forms for www.optoutprescreen.com.
- Complete information for www.donotcall.gov.

_ Check your Credit and Bank account transactions monthly.

_ Shred all personal information you are throwing away, to include junk mail that has your name and address on it.

PART VI: SEMINAR INFORMATION

We can and are willing to provide training at your work place or in a conference setting.
We can also bring this training into any venue where this information will benefit the attendees.

We have specialized training for Law Enforcement in either a two or four hour block format.

We also have training available for the corporate world in either a two or four hour block format.

Please contact us at
www.personalinfoprotection.com
for availability and pricing.

PART VII: WEBSITES

Here is a list of websites mentioned in this book:

50 States, http://www.50states.com.

About Opting Out, http://opt-out.cdt.org/moreinfo.

Annual Credit Report, https://www.annualcreditreport.com/cra/index.jsp

The Baby Thane Foundation, http://www.babythane.com.

Boolean Searches, http://www.lscc.edu/library/guides/boolsea.htm.

BRB Publications, Inc, http://www.brbpub.com/pubrecsites.asp.

Congress.org, http://www.congress.org/congressorg/home.

Consumer Privacy Guide, http://www.consumerprivacyguide.org/law.

Direct Marketing Association, http://www.the-dma.org.

Do Not Call Registry, http://donotcall.com.

Equifax, http://www.equifax.com, 1-800-685-1111.

Experian, http://www.equifax.com, 1-888-397-3742.

Family Educational Rights and Privacy Act (FERPA), http://www.ed.gov.

Federal Citizen Information Center, http://www.pueblo.gsa.gov/call/foia.htm.

Federal Trade Commission, http://www.ftc.gov.

Federal Trade Commission, Avoid ID Theft, http://www.consumer.gov/idtheft.

Google, http://www.google.com.

Innovis, http://www.innovis.com.

Intelius, http://www.intelius.com.

Lexis Nexis, http://www.lexisnexis.com.

My Family, http://www.myfamily.com.

National Do Not Call Registry, https://www.donotcall.gov/default.aspx. 1-888-382-1222

Opt Out Prescreen.com, https://www.optoutprescreen.com.

People Finders, http://www.peoplefinders.com.

Personal Information Protection, http://www.personalinfoprotection.com.

Private Eye, http://www.privateeye.com/processor.asp.

The Privacy Act of 1974, http://www.usdoj.gov/04foia/privastat.htm.

Search Systems, http://www.searchsystems.net.

Social Security Administration, http://ssa-custhelp.ssa.gov.

TransUnion, http://www.transunion.com, 1-800-888-4213.

US Department of Commerce, http://www.export.gov/safeharbor/sh_overview.html.

US Search, http://www.ussearch.com/consumer/index.jsp.

Zabasearch, http://www.zabasearch.com.

REFERENCES

50 States, August 2006, http://www.50states.com.

Annual Credit Report, August 2006, https://www.annualcreditreport.com/cra/index.jsp.

BRB Publications, Inc, August 2006, http://www.brbpub.com/pubrecsites.asp.

Congress.org, August 2006, http://www.congress.org/congressorg/home.

Direct Marketing Association (DMA), August 2006, http://the-dma.org.

Do Not Call Registry, August 2006, http://www.donotcall.com.

Equifax, August 2006, http://www.equifax.com.

Experian, August 2006, http://www.experian.com.

Fair Credit Reporting Act, 15 U.S.C. § 681 et seq. 2004.

Federal Trade Commission, Protecting America's Consumers, August 2006, http://www.ftc.gov.

Federal Trade Commission, Avoid ID Theft, August 2006, http://www.consumer.gov/idtheft.

Federal Trade Commission, National Do Not Call Registry, August 2006, https://donotcall.gov/default.aspx.

Google, August 2006, http://www.google.com.

Gramm-Leach-Biliey Act, S. 1332. 1999.

Innovis Data Solutions, August 2006, http://www.innovis.com.

Intelius, August 2006, http://www.intelius.com.

Lake Sumter Community College, Research Guides, Boolean Search Tips, August 2006, http://www.lscc.edu/library/guides/boolsea.htm.

Lexis Nexis, August 2006, http://www.lexisnexis.com.

Mamma, The Mother of All Search Engines, August 2006, http://www.mamma.com/info/privacy.html.

My Family, August 2006, https://www.myfamily.com.

Opt Out Prescreen.com, August 2006, https://www.optoutprescreen.com.

People Finders, August 2006, http://www.peoplefinders.com.

Private Eye, August 2006, http://www.privateeye.com/processor.asp.

The Privacy Act of 1974, August 2006, http://www.usdoj.gov/04foia/privastat.htm.

Search Systems, August 2006, http://www.searchsystems.net.

TransUnion, August 2006, http://www.transunion.com.

US Search, August 2006, http://www.ussearch.com/consumer/index.jsp.

Zabasearch, August 2006, http://www.zabasearch.com.

ABOUT THE AUTHORS

Sandra Raby has worked as a police officer for 23 years. She has spent time in a variety of assignments, both as an officer and as a supervisor. Sandra is currently working as the administrative sergeant in the Police Chief's office and has been in this position for six years. With this assignment, she is her department's liaison to the Superior Court for the Peace Officer Confidentiality Program. Sandra has earned her Bachelor's Degree in Justice Studies and her Masters Degree in Education Counseling with an emphasis on Human Relations.

Lisa Ruggeri has worked as a Criminal Intelligence Analyst in law enforcement for 15 years. During her career, she has become an expert in researching and locating individuals and suspects for the detectives she works with. Lisa has been teaching law enforcement officers in a variety of topics over the past 6 years. Lisa has earned her Bachelor's Degree in Management and her Masters Degree in Organizational Management.

Sandra and Lisa have a passion for teaching and created a training class that they have presented to their police department's officers. Experiencing first hand the problem the release of personal identifying information has created and seeing the officers' strong desire to want to protect themselves and their families, Sandra and Lisa decided to write this book.

The information presented in his book was originally intended for law enforcement officers. But, the more Sandra and Lisa researched this topic and taught their protection process, the more apparent it became to them that any one could benefit from this information. Once they had this realization, the target audience for this book became the general population. Sandra and Lisa's passion will always be with law enforcement and getting the word out about their protection process to every officer across the country. They also do hope, however, that anyone will be able to take this information and apply it in their life to protect their personal identifying information.

www.ingramcontent.com/pod-product-compliance
Lightning Source LLC
Chambersburg PA
CBHW051054050326
40690CB00006B/712
9781425964689